Dementia Diva

tales and tips from a survivor

This book is dedicated to all the friends who have boosted my flagging energy when I was exhausted and cheered me up with their encouragement to keep going with mum when times got tough. They suffered with me (I was a heavyweight bore for years; no change there, I hear them say ... !) so I think that they too will be feeling relief that my caring role is now over.

Published by Perton Press

ISBN 978-0-9955092-0-7

Typeset by JS Typesetting Ltd, Porthcawl, Mid Glamorgan
Printed and bound in Great Britain by Cambrian Printers, Aberystwyth

In memory of my mother

Contents

Chapter 1

Why write a book about dementia?

Make plans for the kind of life you want to live ... but stay flexible as the unexpected can always happen ...

This didn't start out as a book,
it was initially a personal diary of events ...

Writing a diary was probably part of my coping strategy. It was a form of therapy. We all know laughter makes you feel better. Looking at incidents that happened to mum with humour was my coping mechanism. It helped to deflect the anger and resentment that inevitably came from feeling trapped in a difficult situation. Initially I had expected that this carer role would only be for a year or two; however it went on for nearly a decade. After my mother's death I was freed from my "duties" and able to have some leisure time. Initially I decided to catch up with outings and holidays rather than slaving over a hot keyboard on my own, isolated from life ... but then the realisation set in that if I didn't get on with writing this book whilst the memories were fresh in my mind the diary would gather dust in some drawer and I would forget ...

My thoughts, ideas and experiences about the journey you take looking after someone with dementia could be helpful to others in a similar situation. We can all learn from each other by sharing experiences. I started several years ago when mum was about 91. I put a notebook by the side of my chair in the lounge and jotted down amusing if rather sad incidents that happened with her. Coping with the changes in her and the repercussions for my life was mostly a case of laugh or cry ... being her main carer was a strain that became an even bigger burden when I dwelt on the negatives of the situation ... so I found myself purposefully looking for the amusing angle; just to ease the pressure.

I was just at the age where "mid-life crisis" is the buzz phrase we all use to explain middle aged people doing wild and wacky things that are out of character. Having recently divorced this was just what I had been planning for myself. What fun I was going to have! ... Becoming a carer, experiencing depression, social isolation, lack of money, no holidays for years ... .This was *not* what I had planned ... I was in a difficult situation and I needed to learn to laugh at what was happening to survive.

Caring for someone with dementia is stressful and can take over your life to the point you neglect your own health. Hopefully this little book will encourage those in a similar situation to take care of themselves too. I can recall getting a letter from my local NHS requesting me to go for a mammogram. I filed it away and did nothing. The following year another appointment was also cancelled by me as I was "too busy" with mum, and it took me about 3 years to eventually follow it up. This was a little crazy as there is a high incidence of breast cancer in my family, but my reasoning was that going back and forward to medical appointments for mum took priority in my schedule … in retrospect I can see this way of thinking was silly as I was neglecting myself … so if you are ignoring your own health issues hopefully this book will make you a little more selfish, in a good way.

Why read this book? To find out, just answer the following questions:

1. Do you have someone close to you who suffers from dementia?
2. Are you isolated and depressed, facing years of looking after someone you no longer recognise?
3. Do you find yourself feeling anxious, tearful and desperate with frequent panic attacks when near the person you care for?
4. Have you ever felt like pushing them off a cliff; but you don't fancy spending the rest of your life in prison?

… If you recognise yourself read on.

I loved my mum very much and in many ways we were like best friends … With this illness she became a different person whose behaviour often tested me to the limit … so if *I* had truly **murderous thoughts** about her sometimes; becoming her carer had changed my way of thinking. I readily admit to waking up in a sweat after nightmares in which she lived on, and on and on … ..to the point of getting her telegram from the Queen. If this is how caring for her had affected me, what chance is there for people who are indifferent or even cool about a parent or partner whose deteriorating brain function then puts them through this ordeal that can last many years?

In this book I decided to be honest and share my dark humour about the situation of my caring role with the aim that it might help to lift the **burden of guilt** that shadows the thoughts of many people caring for dementia sufferers …

Your thoughts are not wrong or evil; they are quite natural. There are a lot of us out there and the statistics show that by 2025 there will be over a million people with dementia in the UK …

The odds are most people have a friend or relative touched in some way by this condition. There is a lot of suffering going on behind closed doors. I think sharing a laugh about what happens will help to diffuse the tension and bring a welcome blast of fresh air to a taboo subject.

Chapter 2

Introducing the main characters of this tale

Dementia nibbles away at a personality like holes in a Swiss cheese ...

Introducing the main characters of this tale

The author

My involvement with dementia goes back a long way …

After graduating from university in the late 1970s I took a postgraduate course to qualify as a social worker. Two of my training placements were in old people's homes where I had practical experience of working directly with clients during this course. Both were run by the local authority. One was very traditional and the other was a newly built "state of the art" centre that had special sections for stroke victims and dementia sufferers. They left me with rather scary memories of neglect and mistreatment. I did complain to my college about what I witnessed at the second establishment as I felt the elderly people there needed to be treated with more compassion … the manager of the home was furious and asked for the college to terminate my placement immediately. I'm afraid she had caught me sitting down *talking* to the residents when she thought I should have been cleaning the room. I thought that her priorities were all wrong as the elderly residents were desperate for some attention: forget the dust on her skirting boards! All quite traumatic at the time as the incident jeopardised me achieving my qualification as nobody seems to like whistle blowers.

When I finished my course and was let loose on the public, most of my cases concerned children and I went on to specialise in fostering and adoption for the next 20 years. However for several years in the 1980s I had a mixed caseload of clients, some of whom were families who were looking after relatives with dementia. I saw how their lives were completely dominated by their caring role. There was such a lot of pain and social isolation suffered by these carers and very little could be offered to help them other than getting their relative in to a care home once they had reached the end of their ability to cope.

As an only child myself it was rather frightening to contemplate that I might face this one day; but with both of my parents heavy smokers I consoled myself that *keeping them alive* was going to be *my* challenge … how wrong could I have been in the case of my dear mother! She would be sat there puffing on a fag saying to me that she couldn't imagine living long enough to be a nuisance and I would retort … well, "you can do *anything* to me mum; just make sure you *never* lose your marbles!" Mum actually gave up smoking at the age of 71 when my father died of a smoking related disease. Up to that point she had fervently stated whenever I challenged her that smoking kept you fit; warded off colds etc … strange idea but targeted at shutting me up so she could smoke in peace.

The author

Of course I love her very much but...

Her elderly mother

Sometimes I feel that I haven't got a brain anymore...

The dog

I do my bit to help around the house...

From social worker to artist

In 2005 I "reinvented" myself and started working as an artist as I had always loved painting and drawing. Social work had finally lost its appeal to me as bureaucracy had taken over the profession. I started having a few exhibitions of my work and this led to teaching art for several years; mainly to small groups of adults. I am a natural doodler and found creating cartoons a lot of fun. I made some of them into greetings cards that were quite successful in local shops and amongst my students and friends. Each time that I was writing up a funny episode that had happened with mum in my diary I would start to imagine it as a cartoon ... I dipped my toe in the water at Christmas 2013 when I made mum the star of my card for that year.

I am afraid that it was a case of a 50/50 split between recipients of the card who laughed and found it amusing and those who said it was a bit offensive making fun of mum's illness. When I had shown it to mum she had roared with laughter at it and gave her approval for me to go ahead and print; so I wasn't bothered at the criticism. She knew I was writing this book; but I never got to the point of sharing it with her as it wasn't quite finished when she died.

I was very "politically correct" for twenty years whilst working as a social worker; *acutely* aware of not offending anyone. This book is full of jokes and poking fun at mum and her funny behaviour so it is quite likely to offend lots of people, particularly the sensitive amongst you ... There are a few mentions of poo, so if you are a little squeamish or looking at this book whilst eating your lunch perhaps you need to think again before reading on ... just warning you as I didn't want to compromise by sanitising the truth about dealing with dementia ... sorry!

My elderly mother – What was "Fag Ash Lil" like?

I want to tell you a little about my mother so you can appreciate the gradual loss I have felt of someone who was an inspirational parent. I was very proud of her and in many ways she was like a best friend as we shared many interests. This is the awful thing about dementia. The person loses their personality and there is less you can talk about together. At nearly ninety- five she still lived in her own home with carers four times a day and support from me, but she was nothing like the person she used to be.

In her youth mum was quite a beauty. Green eyes, auburn hair and a lovely hour glass figure. (I've got grey eyes, mousey hair and a flat chest; but we don't make ourselves, do we?) Mum was the middle sister in a family of five girls brought up in the heart of the Yorkshire countryside on a farm. Her father was a vet and

When staying overnight at my house somehow my size 18 extra- long length trousers ended up in mum's wardrobe. The following morning I was sat drinking my tea whilst she was dressing. Mum climbed into them and when she realised they were massive and swimming around her waist with the legs trailing on the floor she let out a wail in horror and called me over to take a look.

"Goodness gracious dear, what's happening to me. I seem to be getting much smaller *very quickly* ... look how big my trousers are on me now!"

I must have still been a bit sleepy as I glanced across and immediately thought oh no; she really *does* have something wrong with her; however seconds later we looked at the label and both fell about laughing.

---

she often wistfully talked to me about how much she would have liked to have been a vet like her father as she had a great passion for animals and used to help him with operations in his practice. Equine surgery was his specialism and mum shared this love of horses; becoming a fearless bareback rider in her youth.

She also mused about her desire to be an airline pilot; but without a formal education she wasn't able to achieve either ambition. Waste of a good brain. The trouble was her parents were rather Victorian and didn't believe in educating girls for a career other than that of a wife. So the girls went to a girls' boarding school with holidays on an isolated five hundred acre farm with very little socialising. World War II catapulted the five sisters out of their cloistered background into the world of work and mum found freedom in jobs such as nursing wounded soldiers, working as a land girl and in a factory printing photographs from pilot reconnaissance flights over enemy territory. She clearly had great fun during the war from the tales she has told me; but that didn't last as she met my father and married him in 1945 ... theirs was a stormy relationship; mainly due to mum being such a flirt and dad being so very jealous ... but I don't want to dwell on that topic as it could be a subject for another book: you never know!

Mum had many of the traditional skills associated with being a good housewife. This was something most of her generation of women aspired to; despite the fact they had only recently been given the vote. Mum was a super cook and a very skilled seamstress. She made dad things like tailored tweed jackets and once in my 20s she made me several sets of gorgeous silky underwear with inserts of delicate lace in various pastel shades. She had green fingers in the garden and was skilled at mending things and DIY. This was a good job as dad hadn't a clue.

When mum stays with me at the weekend I have been letting her sit in on my Yoga practice. She sits on the bedroom chair watching me and clearly enjoys watching me. She keeps telling me how clever I am getting in to the different poses. Mum seems to have forgotten how fantastic she was at Yoga; much better than I am, with my large ungainly frame struggling into the different postures, despite all the fags she smoked!

On a couple of occasions in the last few weeks she has waited until I was relaxing in "corpse" pose with my eyes closed; then leaned over and tickled the soles of my feet or grabbed my big toes. The shock of this has made me jump and lose my concentration. Mum has clearly forgotten how important relaxation is to that phase of the routine. It is just as if she is a naughty toddler. Well from last Sunday morning *she is banned from the room!*

I need peace and tranquillity and above all no interference from her in order to go through my routine and it is unfortunate but she will not leave me alone! She walked up to me when I was laid flat on my back on the floor in "corpse" pose and pushed her smelly-socked foot on my nose and pressed down hard. I jumped in fright as I hadn't heard her move from the chair. I told her off and closed my eyes again and she came back to where I was lying on the floor and did the *same thing again*, but this time there was a really nasty crunching sound from my neck vertebrae ....Oh my God, she has given me a whiplash injury! As she did it for the second time she said "Take that you bitch" ... no, she didn't really. Actually she was really upset she'd hurt me as it had been her idea of a joke.

Mum was a formidable character with strong will power and loads of confidence in her abilities. She taught herself Yoga in the 1960s and ran classes from the lounge in our house way before most people in the west had heard of it. She was very much ahead of the curve in this respect. It was not unusual in our house to be watching TV in the lotus position or standing on our heads. She was still doing shoulder stands in her late 80s but stopped when I got anxious that she might have a stroke!

Mum was a charismatic personality and was someone who inspired great affection in people around her. I may have been an only child but I always shared her with other people who she seemed to "adopt". People who wished she was *their* mum. Weird really, but I just accepted it. I had a "sort of sister" 8 years older than me who lived with our family for years from the age of 15; and a girl 13 years older than me who was the daughter of mum's next door neighbour before I was born who has always felt she was "a cuckoo in the wrong nest". She used to crawl through the privet hedge between their houses to spend time with mum. She even ran away to mum when my parents moved house. The attachment between them was strong and she came to visit mum regularly throughout the last few years of mum's life even though she lives at the other end of the country.

Mum absolutely adored driving and in the 1960s and 70s she would think nothing of many hours at the wheel driving the length of Britain in her Ford Anglia to visit various relatives. She even spent a year or two working as a chauffeur for a wealthy lady. She had to cruise along at about 20 miles an hour in a large black limousine, whilst her passenger sat in the back with a bottle of gin. The elderly lady had a neck injury and mum just had to ignore the toots from other impatient drivers and keep herself calm and Zen-like to cope with driving slowly. This was a big difference to her usual style of driving as her nickname at home was "Stirling Moss" because she drove so fast. Mum's rural childhood on the farm had actually led her to learn driving skills on a tractor decades before her "L plates" and formal lessons.

When I was a teenager mum spent several years running a pet shop in a large shopping precinct. It was over 3 storeys and sold lots of creatures from puppies and exotic fish to snakes. I helped out there after school and at weekends as it was so much fun. I even sat in the window wrapped in a snake as a publicity stunt on one occasion ... where was the NSPCC in those days?

In the later part of her working life she ran a 12 bed unit in an observation and assessment centre for children. These youngsters were in the care system for a variety of reasons such as abuse or neglect – and their short stay in my mum's unit was to enable an assessment to determine their future care. I was very proud of her getting this job as she had been interviewed alongside graduates with relevant qualifications ... her astute understanding of human nature and hobby of armchair psychology impressed her employers. She was always two steps ahead of the kids before something happened and was able to defuse difficult situations however upset or aggressive the youngsters became.

Mum was a good bridge player. She even had the experience of playing opposite the famous film star Omar Sharif in a tournament once at her local bridge club. I recall being very envious of this as it was in his heyday when he was gorgeous! She had a razor sharp intellect; so it has been really distressing over the last

Mum's handbag is often so crammed full I can't pull the zip across. A quick look inside reveals lots of bundles of toilet roll folded up. Unravel them and you mostly find nothing at all; but sometimes there is a half-eaten piece of cake or a sticky, already-sucked sweet.

She definitely has a thing now for tissues and loo roll as these folded bundles have started to appear around the room too on every surface. She isn't incontinent (yet) but is clearly planning ahead and doesn't want to be caught short!

decade noticing her faculties deteriorating. I want to remember her as she used to be and all the lovely times we had together ... and what about her negative personality traits I hear you ask? Well I'm going to keep them to myself as this is meant to be a "glass half full" book of positive thinking!

Katie the dog – An important member of the family ...

Katie was the unintended consequences of a Jack Russell who got a Corgi in the family way. A large litter of puppies resulted and the owner advertised in a local newspaper for families to take them with an appealing photograph of the large litter looking very cute. My parents already had a Doberman, but were always suckers for a wet nose, so they applied and were one of the families chosen.

A strange looking cross breed, Katie lived to over 17 and was a strong little character; not a bit soft, fluffy or cuddly. Although she was small she wasn't a lap dog who enjoyed being petted and stroked on someone's knee. Their Doberman was a very different character. Freedie looked fierce but was soft as butter. She didn't fit anyone's knee as she was almost the size of a small pony; however she adored cuddles and used to put her head in your lap for as much grooming and strokes as you could give her. Sadly she died young of a brain tumour.

Katie on the other hand was a little toughie. She liked adventures and my abiding memories of her are of us searching parks calling for her when she ran off; usually chasing squirrels. She had a way of looking at you that said "no way" when you were trying to get her to behave ... she was wilful and knew better than any of us humans, so it has been fun for me deciding what she might say and do in the different scenarios depicted in my cartoons.

When did I start to become mum's carer?

On reflection it happened very gradually as it does for many carers. The job just sneaked up on me until one day I woke up to the horrifying fact that I was inside an invisible prison that I couldn't escape from. I was in my fifties; just divorced and starting a new life. All in all I was feeling very optimistic about the future and ready for a bit of fun!

I had been dealing with mum's post and organising her paperwork and filling out forms for her for many years already as she hated that sort of thing. I had moved house about 6 miles away from her and I know she felt rather sad that I wasn't nearer. *Her* perfect solution would have been for us to pool our resources and live together … *my* solution was to get my independence back after the divorce. However as the saying goes *"Life is what happens whilst you are making other plans"*.

91 years old today!   *diary entry July 2011*

Flowers, cake with candles, singing Happy Birthday, chocolates and a lovely lunch out … Lots of cards too. Mum is staying at my house and seems to be enjoying herself. I take mum home the next day and that evening on the phone she tells me during our conversation that she's really excited about tomorrow … pause from me

"Why are you excited mum?"
"Well it's my birthday and I'm looking forward to it!"

When I pointed out that we had celebrated her birthday already she seemed genuinely horrified and couldn't remember. Then after a long pause she asked me if we could do it again.

The above incident tallies with other memory lapses when mum is completely unable to remember what she has just done. I joked with a few friends that maybe now I just have to tell her she's been out for a slap up meal and save the expense! … but it make me feel very sad and is also distressing for her too. Her little face just puckers up into a frown of confusion.

I collected her from her Thursday Lunch club meeting a few days ago and whilst we were driving along she got all panicky and said "You better hurry dear as I'm going to be late for lunch!" She had just eaten … how awful and a bit of a shock for me each time something like this happens.

Mum on the beach in the 1960s

Mum really loved the house I moved to and was a fantastic help with the renovations. It was a wreck and needed a complete modernisation. We stripped walls, pulled up lino, took nails out of floors and managed to fill numerous skips together. She was in her mid-eighties and still good with a hammer! An en-suite room was created for a lodger initially to help me pay my bills; however the main occupant for several years turned out to be mum … I certainly hadn't planned that!

Mum would stay with me at weekends. It was difficult as she followed me around like a little shadow and didn't like me leaving the room; so I ended up not even going out for walks on my own as it seemed to upset her. My social life suffered and there was a period when she became difficult and rather bad tempered with me. Luckily that wasn't for long and following a hospital admission where she received treatment for depression she gradually changed into a very sweet old lady and we were bestie mates again. *Yep; the prison doors had shut.*

The realisation of my situation put me into a panic as I just couldn't live the life I wanted to. I cried a lot; I rang friends and relatives and did lots of complaining. I kept thinking why me? I was desperate; just like millions of other carers across the world I felt very trapped and isolated … I recall this as a very bleak time for me. I was so busy yearning to be free of the burden I felt had been hoisted on me unfairly by fate … Why hadn't I grasped by middle age that life *isn't* fair to most of us in some way or another. After floundering around for a long time feeling sorry for myself, I realised I just wasn't *thinking* properly.

I found myself sitting opposite my GP sobbing my eyes out at one stage about 3 years ago; desperate for help as I thought I was on the verge of a nervous breakdown. In between bouts of blowing my nose and wiping the tears away I remember going on and on to her about my "wasted life" … I had a good degree, lots of skills and potential yet I was trapped in a lowly role of care giver … I whined on about how unfair this was as I felt it was sapping all my energy year in year out … How could this have happened to me? To give my GP credit she listened and was really very supportive. I was in there so long that day a big queue formed in the waiting room. I came out with a prescription to relieve the anxiety, a referral to a support group and also for one-to-one counselling: all three things were quite helpful in eventually getting me back on track.

> # Can't change the situation? … so change your *attitude* to it

Apart from taking drugs to quell the anxiety and depression another way to survive the role of carer is teach yourself to think differently. It is too easy to slip into negativity. I am lucky in having good pals who tick me off when I get too down and start thinking life is bleak as they know this isn't helping. "Mindfulness" is a buzz word at the moment and there are plenty of books and articles that guide you in re-programming your patterns of thinking. I also read up about the Buddhist philosophy and went to meditation classes which were extremely helpful. My local health authority ran some tutorials on cognitive therapy that was very interesting and helpful in re-programming some of my behaviour to enable me to feel more relaxed and positive.

Situations don't create emotions – it is the *thoughts* we have about those situations that determine how we feel. Negative thoughts can be very destructive to our wellbeing so you need to try and work out a *different way of thinking.*

> # Can't live the life you want?
> # Work at loving the life you live.

The reality is that over the years my mum had gradually turned from a strongly opinionated feisty woman into a very sweet gentle and charming personality. She always gave profuse thanks for everything that I did for her and was polite and very appreciative. This made it easier for me to continue my caring role when it became so demanding. I now realise this is *incredibly lucky* as it must be devastating if the person you have to care for becomes difficult and aggressive towards you; a painful situation that is not uncommon. There is so much raw emotion involved in caring for a parent or partner with dementia. You are just *too* close and it can be so very painful watching them deteriorate in front of your eyes.

> *Handbag contents are fascinating ...*   *diary entry 2011*
>
> *Today I've found chocolate biscuits in the bottom of her bag, all broken and melted; 3 pairs of nail scissors and dozens of sachets of Demerara sugar: some tatty and ripped and spilling their sticky grains into her bag ... there is also lots and lots of folded tissues, toilet paper and napkins ... literally dozens of them packed in tightly ... real origami jobs! I started to unravel some of them and realised that inside wrapped up like an Egyptian mummy were objects: a lump of cake going mouldy, a half sucked boiled sweet ... mostly food items lovingly stored away for when she was peckish.*
>
> *"Put a bit of lippy on mum, it'll brighten up your face" She fumbles in her bag and brings out her purse ... "no, that's not your lipstick mum" She fishes in again and pulls out her blue plastic inhaler. "Is this it dear?" ... "no mum; that's not your lipstick either" ... maybe third time lucky ... "no, that's your comb mum". Give me your bag and I'll get it for you ... what fun!*

In the last few months of her life as her dementia progressed mum said very little to me. She used to occasionally comment that she didn't think she's got a brain anymore. However she used to regularly say things like: "Darling, I just don't know what I did to deserve you looking after me so well". I always gave the obvious answer like" You were a lovely mum, blah, blah blah ... " However simultaneously the reply in my head was often something *quite different ...* I'll leave it to your imagination ...

20

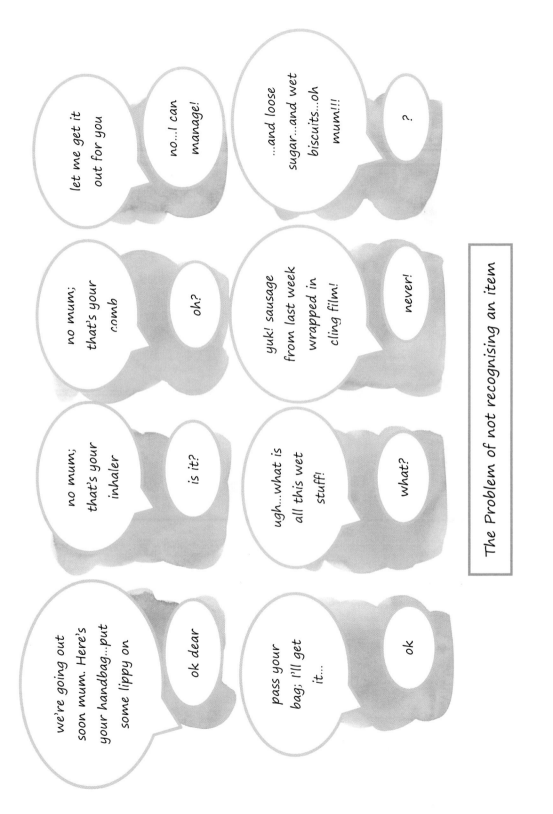

The Problem of not recognising an item

Where has this new sense of humour come from?   diary entry 2011

Mum likes Danish pastries, particularly the circular ones in a swirl pattern filled with cinnamon and raisins. I bought her one as a treat with her cup of coffee in a café and she sat patiently unwinding it from the outside and eating it very slowly bit by bit in a methodical way until it was about half the original size … but still perfectly circular.

After about 10 minutes of this activity mum leant over to me and said: "You're going to have to take this back dear as it is *far* too small. What a cheek they've got selling it to you at the counter. You need to complain and get them to swop it for a proper sized one!"

I don't know this woman; she is an imposter. My mum never had much of a sense of humour and this lady is often really funny.

Chapter 3

Caring and coping strategies

You can't change the situation, but you can change the way you are thinking about it ...

Caring and coping strategies

Guilt–sorry, as a carer you can't avoid it!

I am sorry to tell you this but *whatever* you do *you will feel guilty*; especially if you are female. We are programmed to be empathetic and relationship orientated. You can rationalise to yourself that you never really got on with them; that you don't owe them anything as your relationship with them was not good: they were a crap parent or partner … you don't owe them any respect. However the fact that you are reading this book at all shows me that you *are* interested in looking at ways to cope with your feelings.

I have known many people, both as a professional and as a friend, who have had a parent suffering from dementia in a care home for years. It is clear that you cannot avoid the pain of seeing the inevitable deterioration dementia brings. Out of sight is definitely *not* out of mind as there is the constant worry of what is happening to them when you are not there. We are hard-wired to feel guilty however good the establishment is at caring for them.

A brilliant invention …   *2009–2011*

"Am I going to your house this weekend dear?"
"Yes mum, you come to me every weekend"
"Oh good … Are the seats booked in the cinema?"
"Yep; front row, best in the house as always"

… We arrive and mum resumes her seat on the sofa and puts her feet up, the telly goes on and it is "cinema conditions" for the rest of the day. I've discovered that flat screen TVs are brilliant for minding grannies just as much as they are for toddlers … a real blessing for stressed out carers!

The worst times for me have been when my mother had two prolonged stays in hospital, as a change of environment can be very disorientating to someone suffering from dementia. Each time there was the inevitable deterioration in her behaviour. On both occasions once back in her own home she improved; but the down side of that was that I had to persuade the medical team that she was able to cope at home; despite her vulnerability. On the second occasion after a fall she required an operation on her hip and leg. This was a difficult task as they would have far rather she had moved from hospital into a residential home. They thought she needed 24 hour care, however I knew she slept very soundly and could manage with just daytime carers. It was hard taking the responsibility for this decision; but I felt I needed to give her a situation with a little risk involved to ensure that she still had a sense of her own dignity and control over her life. It was difficult arguing the case for giving her this chance at independent living; but luckily for me it worked out well.

It is my view that you have to steel yourself to live with a certain amount of *risk* when deciding on care for someone with dementia. We were very lucky as in my mum's case she had carers who went in to her home four times a day to look after her. Also once she stopped reading she began watching TV as her main pastime. Mum called it "cinema conditions" since she had a new big digital flat screen TV with subtitles she could follow ... settling down with wall to wall detective drama re-runs was her idea of heaven!

Buddhist philosophy certainly helps with the concept of dealing with guilt. In relation to feeling guilty in your caring role it is inevitable that things will go wrong and you may blame yourself. However it is important to accept that you should only feel guilty if you do something really evil with the intent of causing harm. Most of the time when you are feeling guilty you are just punishing yourself for caring too much and being fallible. You are only human and often very tired, so no wonder you might feel pressurised as if you need to split yourself in two to get the jobs done.

> # Remember that you aren't useful unless you keep fit ... only then can you do the job of caring effectively!

I think we need to regard the person we are looking after with a sort of "detached compassion"; you love the person and they matter a lot to you but you keep that awareness of death. This thought that none of us are eternal and that they will not be here forever will make us appreciate and enjoy them whilst we have them with us; it isn't tragic or pessimistic – just realistic and life-enhancing. I recognise that in our culture we do seem to shy away from this subject. I am not religious myself so I can cherry pick ideas from other cultures which I find helpful.

I have been down the path of howling at the moon and berating my fate as a carer ... and where did it get me? Yes, palpitations and high blood pressure.

Funnily enough looking back I can now see that the last few years of caring have had many positive aspects. These are the things I have to meditate on and value; not least the amount of time I was able to spend with mum. I have learned patience and tenacity. I have learned to slow down and be far less of a perfectionist. Passable is now good enough, so I don't beat myself up too much when I can't get all the tasks done. I certainly appreciate the importance of good friends as they have been a lifeline to me when I felt down.

This is a 21st century epidemic of a disease where GP's and hospital doctors are learning on the job. There are gloomy predictions everywhere in the media about this challenging demographic "time-bomb" … .so if we can't avoid it we need to learn to live with the reality. A change in our attitudes would help. OK; so you've got arthritis in your hip joint and after years of hobbling around in pain you need a replacement joint. Everyone around you understands and sympathises. A bit of your body has failed, but treatment can put it right … no stigma to this problem. However if it is your *brain* that fails you; well that is a very different matter. Many of us are facing seeing once capable independent parents or partners turn into toddlers … and our deepest darkest fear is that we may eventually be sufferers too.

> # I can see now that there is *"no gain in pulling at the chains"* … learn to live in captivity

Unfortunately there is very little prestige in dealing with the elderly; so there are not enough doctors interested in dedicating their lives to becoming Psychogeriatric Consultants. My mum was very lucky as she *did* get a full assessment of her condition as a hospital in-patient several years ago by one of these rare consultants and their team of mental health professionals. This was crucial in determining the role that urinary tract infections and depression were having on her dementia. Sorting out these problems made a massive difference to her ability to think clearly and her mood. There need to be many more of these specialists.

The progression of dementia is not easy to chart as each individual sufferer is unique. Medical staff can give you a prognosis; although deterioration of the person's faculties and ability to manage their lives is inevitable, the *quality* of that life and of yours as their carer *is* something you *can* affect … by your *attitude to the situation.*

Ability to learn new things

As mentioned before it is difficult for doctors to predict the progress of dementia. There are so many different types and the medical profession seems to be just at the beginning of understanding what happens to the brain of sufferers. Equally every sufferer is different in terms of their background, current environment, mental agility, etc. I have known friends and colleagues whose parents began to suffer in their fifties; yet others like my mother who didn't show signs until they were in their mid-eighties. Then we have individuals like my mum's neighbour who lived to be 103, was as bright as a button and only stopped doing the Times crossword a short time before her death.

There are predictive questionnaires used by medical staff to assess how much memory someone has lost. When mum took these tests I was very upset when told her results were not good. However I am a determined person and when I they said mum had lost the ability to learn to walk again or manage her Zimmer frame after she had been hospitalised following a fall I was reluctant to accept it. They didn't want to give her time to learn ... this was a luxury and she was blocking a bed in hospital. The physiotherapists and the doctors felt that she was better off going straight to a care home from hospital; but I stuck to my gut feeling that once she was safely back in her own home and not nervous or distressed she *would learn the skills* necessary to manoeuvre her frame and live independently again.

It took several months of negotiations to convince the medical staff, the physiotherapist and the social worker to give her a home trial ... thank goodness they eventually agreed as she regained her mobility and was able to return home for a further 3 years despite their scepticism. They are very risk adverse as understandably they don't want to get sued, and it was down to me to take the gamble.

Every individual learns differently ... some respond to verbal instructions whilst others do better with diagrams or demonstrations. Mum was fine with the written word, but I also made a few drawings of the exercises the physiotherapists wanted her to do several times a day and this really helped get her on track with recuperating ... just try things and see what works.

Mum was 92 at this point, but I knew with lots of work we could get her brain neurons firing off on different pathways to get her moving again ... I wasn't happy with the social worker mum was allocated in hospital as she had wanted me to agree to moving in with mum on a 24hr basis if she was allowed home. I knew this wasn't necessary as she was a very sound sleeper. (Also I knew I would go crazy

Dear mum you MUST do what the physiotherapist girls tell you and exercise your legs every hour during the day…in bed or when you are in your chair…no excuses!

1. rotate each of your ankles one way and then another

2. now point your foot – flex it as if you are a ballet dancer (bit late for a change in career!)

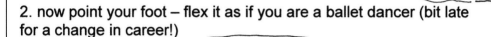

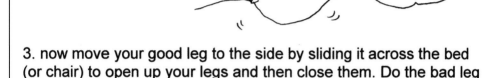

3. now move your good leg to the side by sliding it across the bed (or chair) to open up your legs and then close them. Do the bad leg too. …you saucy madam; I said close your legs!

4. Bend your good knee and slide your leg up the bed using your tummy muscles…now do the bad leg.

5. You can now congratulate yourself for being brave as I know it hurts…so to end your exercises raise your arms in the air and swirl them about a bit…use the bed or the arms of the chair and raise your body up on your arms to get them strong again….phew! Now you can have a chocolate éclair to celebrate!

Love Jane X

within the first week …) Luckily I had my request for a change of caseworker accepted. This new professional was key to the plans being formulated for mum to return to her own home for a trial period with proper care support 4 times a day. Mum had several small steps to negotiate within the ground floor of her home and also a rather narrow doorway … I had my fingers crossed and I felt really sick with nerves the first few days she was back home … but it worked! Mum was more relaxed and able to concentrate on developing the skills she needed. It took several months before she was confident in moving around but in time she began to use her Zimmer just like it was a racing car. "Sterling Moss" was back!

The last straw … problems with water

Looking after someone with dementia is often about thinking outside the box for solutions to problems. Like a lot of dementia sufferers mum had an aversion to water and getting washed. Lots of coaxing was required! Also mum had had

---

Sore bums need soft cushions   diary entry September 2012

Since coming out of hospital in June mum has had a delicate "rear end". Thin skin and incontinence have caused this problem. I decided that she needed one of those nice soft inflatable cushions you get from the chemist. The ones offered by the district nurse and social services physiotherapy department seemed a bit hard on her delicate arthritic coccyx.

Mum was waiting in the car outside the chemist shop so I took the cushion out to show her to see if she wanted to try it.

"It looks very useful dear" she said

I asked her if she thought it would be comfortable to sit on and she replied:

"Oh definitely darling; I think *you'll* find it *very* comfortable" was her reply

No mother **it isn't** for me it is for **you!** I said in exasperation

"Oh I don't need it dear; but I think *you* might find it helpful came the reply.

The thought that went through my head at that moment was that *she* may have the sore arse; but *I'm* the one with the headache!

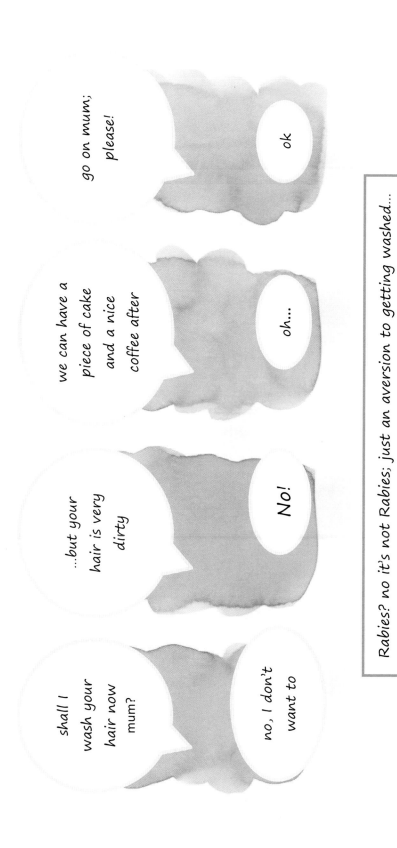

Rabies? no it's not Rabies; just an aversion to getting washed...

a problem regarding drinking liquids for years. You'd think you were giving her poison. It had truly driven me to distraction as it meant she was often constipated and a little dehydrated. This is a dangerous combination for brain function in anyone. Repeated urinary tract infections can play havoc with general health and need to be avoided by keeping up fluid intake. Easier said than done I hear you say.

With mum I instigated a diluted glass of sugar free cranberry juice every morning and called it "her medicine". The carers put it out for her and we all encouraged her to have drained the glass by mid-afternoon. Cranberries have been found to contain high levels of a chemical that prevents bacteria responsible for infections sticking to the bladder wall. It seemed to work on her so it might be worth trying in liquid or pill form if this is a problem you face rather than resorting to repeated courses of antibiotics.

I had a "eureka moment" when pouring yet another cup of cold tea she hadn't touched down the sink. Why not try her with a straw? Might she find it easier and more enjoyable to drink this way? I know they are for cold liquids like juice and milkshakes, but it worked with her a treat. Instead of battling to make her take a sip she seemed to enjoy the feeling and found it easier ... Why hadn't I thought of this before?! I experimented with different widths of straw and tried nice brightly coloured ones to see which she liked best ... at least she was drinking more at last.

Hugs and the power of touch

We all know how relaxing and therapeutic a massage can be; whether you have paid for a session from a professional therapist or it is a partner or friend loosening up your shoulders after a hard day ... touch can be magical. This is not surprising considering the skin is our largest organ and it is crammed with nerve endings that send messages to the brain when stimulated.

It seemed to soothe mum when I brushed her hair or stroked her head when I was styling it. I reckon it is the fundamental "grooming behaviour" that many animals use to reinforce bonds. With my bad back I found it difficult to bend down to give mum a cuddle in her chair or when she was lying in bed ... I ended up giving her a cuddle when she stood up; so her head often seemed to be by my waist. It *looked* funny, *felt* weird, but did the job and she *enjoyed* it. Touch ... Make sure there is enough of it ... and if you can't, a rub down with a flannel and then a towel is a good substitute!

Periodically over the years mum and I had little "foot massage sessions" when we would work on each other's feet. We didn't really know what we were doing; we would just get a bowl of warm water to soak the feet in, dry them off nicely on a soft towel and then slather them in a delicious smelling foot cream and get digging in! A quick flick through a reflexology book gave us a little guidance and the results were always good.

Mum had always been tottering around in shoes with high heels with pointed toes when she was younger. We are a family with square fat feet so inevitably her poor toes had been squashed and damaged by fashion. Flexing and stretching her toes in these sessions often made her squeal in pain at the beginning: however after I had done the full massage she said they felt much better. Torture maybe, but it worked … I mean, I enjoyed it!

As mentioned previously, with the onset of dementia mum had developed an aversion for water and washing generally. A few years ago it was a big challenge for me to get her to let me give her a weekly shower and hair wash. It used to be quite a battle as she didn't want to get wet. In the last few years however she became more passive and I continued to do sessions on her feet every few weeks so I could also keep her toenails short. Unfortunately poor circulation in her feet meant that I had to be extremely gentle as the skin was fragile.

Mum didn't have a bathroom downstairs in her house, so all washing took place with a bowl of warm water, liquid soap for new babies, (anything else would be too harsh), flannels and a towel. I am convinced that mum benefited a great deal from the daily body wash the carers gave her on getting her out of bed. The washing and drying with a towel stimulated her skin and I reckon it was very important to her general health. They paid particular attention to her poor feet and I think without this her ability to walk would have been compromised.

A hairy tip for carers

When I was a little girl I wanted to be a hairdresser when I grew up. Every birthday and Christmas I would ask for a doll with long hair as a present. A Sindy doll or a Tressy with the long pull out pony tail didn't last long with me as I got busy with the scissors. I had a collection at one stage of about 20 bald dolls with severe crew cuts. I just adored playing with hair. My Godmother had long hair down to her waist worn in a plaited bun. She was a gem and used to let me comb it for her. What fun I had. Now my mum was a real spoilsport as far as I was concerned. She never let me *near* her hair. It was always beautifully coiffured and she never left the house on a morning without spending at least half an hour

BAD

Before
Arrival
of
Dementia

immaculate
make-up and hair
beautifully cut

MAD

Mum
Altered
by
Dementia

wind tunnel style
hairdo and wild
eyebrows

SAD

Sorted !
Accepting
of
Dementia

cheeky short hairdo
gelled into shape in
seconds...and no
eyebrows!

curling it with tongs or rollers in front of her special 3 way mirror. This was a daily ritual. I would even go so far as to say it was an obsession of hers as it had to be perfect.

With the onset of her dementia however she was at my mercy at last! No, I didn't given her a crew cut or make her grow it in to a long plait. I had actually achieved my dream and became a hairdresser. Her personal hairdresser; and she loved it. I cut her hair, washed it and curled it for her … and it never looked better! We always went through a ritual every time I got her ready to go out. Fluffing her hair with styling mouse; putting some nice perfume on her wrist and behind her ears, sorting a nice pair of clip-on earrings to match her jumper and *always* a nice bit of lippy to brighten up her face. This was important as it involves lots of touching and attention that made her feel good … no wonder she was still flirting when we were out together! The invention of hair styling mousse revolutionised getting her ready to go out anywhere. A few seconds scrunching a ball of white foamy mousse in her locks and a little tease and tweak with my fingers and her very straight hair fell into lots of soft curls … a miracle for the girl who had memories of sitting around bored stiff waiting for what seemed hours for her mum to be ready.

I wonder if that funny "mouse" stuff would work on my fur?

Chapter 4

Depression

dementia sufferer and their carers
(dog too; as all family members are affected)

often overlooked by families; and even the
medical profession miss this too ...

Depression
Dementia sufferer and their carers
(dog too; as all family members are affected)

Depression in people with dementia

...don't forget me!

I was a qualified social worker yet I had totally missed the signs that my mother was suffering from depression in her eighties. It was her GP that picked this up and suggested she had "the blues". Often it is those who are closest who can miss the signs completely. Guilt again I'm afraid! Mum just couldn't get over the death of her youngest sister with whom she had been extremely close. Even though they lived hundreds of miles apart they had spoken on the phone several times a day for many years. I could always tell it was her sister on the other end of the phone if I walked in the room as mum would be roaring with laughter as her sister Joyce was such a character, always making fun out of nothing much. The loss mum felt clearly dragged her down and even five years later she was suffering. From hearsay about other people's elderly relatives I reckon depression is a massively under-diagnosed problem for the elderly. In certain cases of dementia depression is also part of the picture; and when this is treated the individual will function far better ... but I think this is often missed, even by the medical profession.

> ## someone with dementia might *also* be suffering from depression ... this can be overlooked

OK, with our 21st century progress in medicine we are keeping our population in the prosperous west alive for a lot longer. This is admirable. However what we have to ask ourselves is this: don't they deserve to be relaxed and content in their last few years? Getting older is often all about loss: failing eyesight and hearing, partners, friends and relatives dying before them and worst of all the loneliness suffered by so many elderly people living with very little social contact ... sounds an attractive prospect doesn't it?

So checking out whether depression is part of the problem with the person you are caring for *might* be useful as there are drugs that would help. As someone who never even wanted to take an aspirin for a headache this is an interesting turnaround, but the difference between mum with anti-depressants and without them was amazing. She was taken off them when in hospital being treated after a fall and quickly reverted to spitting out food and being difficult.

Depression in carers

As a carer I experienced anger and frustration on a daily basis often mingled with a great despair and sadness at the gradual loss of the personality I knew.

"Poogate"   *entry Christmas Day 2014*

Having flu and a chest infection for over 3 weeks now I was feeling a little tired before I turned up at mum's house today to cook the turkey lunch for the two of us. I had already psyched myself up to make it an enjoyable meal ... optimistic as ever! It turned out that mum had a bad episode on Christmas Eve and had been found by the night time carer stripped naked with poo all over her; on her chair, on the floor on her cream fluffy rug and with a lump in her glass of water on the table. This meant loads of washing to do and shampooing of the pale pink carpet (yes, I know. But this carpet was in the house when mum was extremely careful and house proud. Lino may be more practical, but it isn't the same and I don't think she would like it) I had to disinfect surfaces everywhere.

The funniest thing was that I couldn't find the loose cover from mum's chair anywhere in the house ... it wasn't in the pile of soiled bed linen, so where was it? Puzzled I search around the house. Then as a last resort I decided to look in the outside wheelie bin. If any of mum's neighbours had looked out of their windows at this time they would have seen me hanging over the edge of the bin wearing my yellow rubber gloves sorting through rubbish in a freezing cold wind. Lo and behold it was in there tied up in a rubbish bag with kitchen waste ... .the carer had thrown it away!! I was delighted to find the cover and after a couple of washes it was good as new and fine to go back on the chair a few days later. The carer must think we are made of money to chuck it out like that! Mum seemed blissfully unaware of the jobs I was doing today. I managed to stay sane and still cooked a turkey lunch for 2.30pm. Now that is positive thinking! Of course mum didn't do it ... "Smearing poo? Don't be ridiculous dear!"

43

If you are lucky you will have a wide support network of friends and relatives around you to help you cope, but more usual is the gradual social isolation that sometimes you unwittingly create yourself by withdrawing from society. Make the effort to visit friends for a little chat occasionally, as over the years they might become far less inclined to visit you, particularly if you live with the person with dementia as it stresses them out.

So if you recognise that this negative slide into the carer role is isolating you and making you depressed, you need to address the problem and *do something about it* … Get some help from your GP to see if medication might help you cope. For some carers joining an exercise class or a walking group gives them some space to relax. You *must* build in time for yourself somehow as the caring role is exhausting. There are support groups popping up in every community … and if there isn't one for you maybe you could start one!

that's strange...
I can't see her in
her chair...

Chapter 5

Mum's memory loss

"ignorance is bliss" ... sometimes!

Mums' memory loss

Cooking skills

With my mum the first signs that I noticed she was suffering from memory loss were when she was in her eighties and had forgotten how to cook our favourite spaghetti sauce one day. She had always been a super cook producing tasty food from scratch on a daily basis. Roasts, trifles, Italian and Chinese stir fries ... just a lovely repertoire of delicious food. She asked me to write the spaghetti recipe out for her to follow which was surprising. A few days later I found a large pan in the fridge full of the most gruesome sticky mixture that was clearly inedible. Over the next year it was apparent that she was creating some wild and wacky meals that were rather unappetising so I took over most of the cooking. Unfortunately at this time her appetite was also dwindling and she was losing weight.

The no-cook method   *diary entry 2011*

Gone are the days when mum would cook herself proper meals. I think she has just forgotten how to prepare food; even simple snacks. I mainly catch her eating wholemeal toast and honey with jam or cheese when I call on her. I now realise that when I do succeed in cajoling her in to eating soup too on the days she isn't going out to a hot meal; she doesn't heat it up in a pan, she just takes a spoon into the lounge and eats it cold out of the tin. She's like a teenager again!

Mum eats out 3 or 4 times a week and is delighted she hardly has any washing up, so I mustn't get too anxious ...

I just love cooking and having vast pig-outs over home- cooked meals. This was one thing mum and I loved to do together until dementia completely ruined her appetite. Apart from things like egg on toast I must admit that it has been many years since I slaved over a hot stove to produce a nice meal for us both as I couldn't bear her turning away the food I produced. So for the last six or seven years I took her out to the pub or a restaurant for a meal instead; as at least then it didn't feel like a personal rejection when she only ate a few mouthfuls of what was on her plate.

It really is a case of learning as you go along as what suits one person will not work for another. Mum became rather strange about putting an average spoon or fork full of food in her mouth. She only wanted child size cutlery and preferred a teaspoon to eat her pudding. This is why it could take hours for her to get through a small meal … a real tooth grinding experience for me as my jaw set whilst I watched her excruciatingly slow progress.

I *could* have and really *should* have looked at this slow eating quite differently of course. Remember it is *your attitude* to what is happening that matters.

I needed to remind myself that mum was a follower of Yoga. She had always been an advocate of masticating each mouthful properly before swallowing, at least 20 chews a mouthful until it becomes liquid and digestion starts in the mouth. This is what Yogis believe to be very important to health. When I was a child she often used to tell me off for bolting my food. Yes, it had become very extreme with her as she was so very slow; far better that I just finished my plate of food and then buzzed off to do some jobs rather than watching her. Not good table manners, but hey ho.

Driving her car

Mum moved to north London from the Midlands a few years before she became ill and I was very proud of the way she had learned the roads around her home in order to drive to the shops, her friend's houses, social events and her local pub for lunches out. We had re-mortgaged her house in order to buy her a new car and she was extremely proud of it. As she was quite elderly I tried to get her to accept an automatic gear box, however she was adamant that she needed to "feel the gear changes" and that she wanted to drive her car properly. Needless to say mine is an automatic.

She was fine with her new car for a couple of years; however one day she was taking me somewhere as a passenger and I was horrified to realise that she had forgotten how to change gears using the clutch. Lots of nasty grating noises and a very red-faced mum (terrified passenger too). Mum admitted that she had lost her confidence at the wheel and not long afterwards we sold her beloved car as we both realised she wasn't safe driving anymore as her memory was failing fast. This was very traumatic for mum as driving had been something she absolutely loved.

Mum still adored cars; however in the last few years she had her own chauffeur (me). She loved going out for a drive even if it was just a short journey to the local café. I had to keep my cool as she repeatedly said to me: "You're a really good driver darling" about four or five times even on a short trip. This was a bit annoying … but I just kept smiling …

Having a good pluck

No the above isn't a typing error! Mum did not cook, read the Times or play bridge any more ... but there is one thing she still loved to do that had been a major hobby since adulthood ... and that was plucking! The women in our family are extremely hairy. Daily sessions with a magnifying mirror is the only thing that keeps us from having a full bushy beard moustache and mono brow. Mum may have lost the art of making a cup of tea but she still loved a good session with her tweezers!

The one difference was that it became open season on any hairs that appeared on her face; and that includes eyebrows ... so she didn't have any. Quite a wise move really as they had started to grow several inches long and had become very wild and wiry, poking into her eyes making them water ... so they got the treatment too.

Losing memory of who she was

Mum always insisted she was "big boned", not fat. She had a full figure in her 60s and 70s and at 5ft 5ins and weighing in at between 11 and 12 stone this meant elasticated waist bands and high blood pressure. Her sisters used to joke that she was unable to pass a bakery without buying a big box of cream cakes. On doctor's orders she was put on a diet where she had to cut out the double cream, cheese, sweets, etc. until she successfully got down to a good weight when she was in her early eighties. She had never dieted in her life before and she stuck religiously to their advice sheet that worked a treat. However once she was in her nineties I decided she could eat whatever she fancied ... I wasn't going to be the one to spoil her fun.

Food is often a big issue to handle with dementia sufferers for some barely eat or drink at all like my mum; whilst others eat too much. They forget they have eaten a meal and carry on wanting more food. Dealing with this change is a real challenge for the carers, whichever way the brain has been affected by dementia.

As mentioned before my mum's appetite changed dramatically with the onset of dementia, so began a decade of coaxing her to eat during which she shrank to a tiny little figure with no flesh on her bones. The interesting thing is how mum's perception of her body changed as she completely forgot that she had ever been fat.

When I arrived at mum's house this morning mum's carer was in a really agitated state. She greeted me with: "I've been trying to get you on the phone. Your mum has had an accident" She is only a young girl barely out of her teens and as I went white with shock she blurted out ... "No, it's OK, nothing serious. It's just she had diarrhoea in the night and it is all over her bed and the carpet." I held my breath and entered the room to find mum sat on her commode as if butter wouldn't melt.

The carer had already put the soiled bed linen in the wash; however she had missed mums bed socks that were absolutely caked in diarrhoea ... so I picked them up and held them at arms' length whilst whisking them into the kitchen to the machine with the rest of the washing ... then I stopped a minute as I was puzzled as to why there was no smell at all (I couldn't hold my breath for ever) Poo should smell shouldn't it??

I lifted the sock to my nose and all I could smell was chocolate; with maybe a nice hint of caramel. Going back in the room to the distraught carer I noticed that under mum's bed was an empty wrapper of Cadbury's caramel. Mum had taken it to bed with her and had been munching on it during the night. I realised she must have fallen asleep with squares of it getting plastered to her pyjamas; slowly melting and getting all over the bed. She must have got it on her bed socks and then gone to the loo in the night, squashing it into the pale pink carpet. The delicious liquid caramel centres had stuck in the fibres of the carpet to such an extent I needed get on my knees with a knife to scrape it off ... but it wasn't diarrhoea and it wasn't an emergency ... but it was hysterically funny ... once I'd recovered from the clearing up!

This became apparent when a few years ago we were looking through an old photo album together. Mum pointed to one of the photographs of herself and asked me "goodness; who is that fat pig?" ... a few photos later she exclaimed again "that person needs to sew her mouth up!" Mum was full of indignation when I suggested that she was looking at herself ... "no ... no ... Never I've *always been slim!* That's *not* me in those photographs!" I can recall being quite shocked that she couldn't recognise herself. I decided that regular sessions with albums of photos would be beneficial and that had proved to be the case as she could often name most of the family members, including herself with these regular viewings, and really enjoyed the conversations this activity prompted between us.

Chapter 6

The use of memory prompts

whatever turns them on ...

The use of memory prompts

Labels and diagrams

On your shopping list you need: black felt tip pen, white card, sticky pads and/
or celloptape

Visual recognition of objects, even when they are in clear view to everyone else,
can be a problem for dementia sufferers. Mum's peripheral vision was not good
but it still didn't explain how she went to pick her lipstick out of her handbag and
came out with her inhaler. Making sure important items are displayed clearly in
an accessible place is very important. If something is put away in a cupboard it
is truly "out of sight out of mind". I wrote out instructions for mum on pieces of
card using a broad tipped felt pen and taped them to various surfaces all over the
house. No capital letters and clearly written out. For example:

> **answer the phone mum when
> the yellow light flashes**

> **Mum please don't lock this
> door as the carers can't get in!**

> **switch the TV off when
> you go to bed**

As I already mentioned my mum loved her new wide screen TV. However when
it was delivered she was a little confused with the different control panel. The
answer came when I drew it on a sheet of A4 card and put it on the table by
her chair. Each important button had a tag, so she was better able to follow
how to change channels. She still got stuck occasionally; but as I also had a
diagram in my own house I could talk her through her mind block on what to do
... problem solved and so enjoying her favourite programmes was still able to be
an important part of her life ... detective stories or any kind of court room drama
usually had her engrossed.

Mum can't hear the telephone ringing anymore. She really has become deaf as a post. I ordered a signal system of a yellow flashing light and amplifier fixed to the line a few months ago and it worked fine for a while, then one day I realised that she can't see the flashing light anymore as it is in the wrong place on the side where she has less vision. This was a Eureka moment as I just have to move it to the side of her good eye. No ... it isn't working, so I write out a large sign and stick it to the table in front of her chair.

"When the yellow light flashes mum answer the phone"

I asked her to read what I'd put and it is clear the lettering was too small ... try again. Still too small.

With a bit of patience and a few goes the lettering on the sign is now about 4 inches big in thick black felt pen, but she can read it ... .we're in business again and she is answering the telephone ... result!

Written instructions for care workers

If you go down the same path as mum and I did, it will mean getting carers in to help at some stage. However thoroughly your care plan is developed you will probably find that notes on cupboards, on the fridge, on doors and tables will be needed to make sure the carers follow what the person being cared for wants to be done. For example I had notes on mum needing her cardigan on whatever the weather, and by the drinks cupboard to say she liked her drinks very weak with 2 sugars ... that sort of thing. The carers were often in a hurry to do all the tasks and I knew they found this helpful. The dining room table was stacked with all her medication and several different types of incontinence pads with notes to make sure they could see which ones to use at a glance ... Let's face it, no one came to dinner parties there anymore!

You might find that paid carers are on a sort of "automatic pilot" when they are going through the caring tasks to the extent that they can sometimes not notice a label on a jumper and put it on back to front, almost garrotting the little neck inside ... same with pants too and I have often gone from being really annoyed when I've found mum trussed up and unable to move her legs freely to laughing at the absurdity of it all in the space of a few moments when mistakes like that were discovered. What was so sad for me in the last year or so was that mum didn't notice herself.

...or jumper; as both happened occasionally

Regular telephone calls

For years I telephoned mum regularly throughout the day to have a little chat and remind her to go to the toilet. I tried to time it for key points in the day between carers' visits as I knew once mum got involved in watching a drama on the telly she would not move out of her chair unless prompted. On average I probably called her about four or five times a day. However in her last year of life she started falling asleep and not answering like she used to do; this meant my anxiety over her was even greater than before. Mum didn't seem to have noticed the difference herself; but it meant more wet pairs of trousers for the washing!

What day is it today?

Quite a few years ago before mum had carers helping her she began to have difficulty remembering what day it was and whether she was going out or doing a particular activity. She was also administering her own medication. She had always kept a small diary in her handbag for reference and to put in social events; however this wasn't useful enough when it came to orientate her to what the day was (Monday, Tuesday, Wednesday …) and also what part of the day she was currently in and whether she had to go out at some point in the day and whether it was time to take her pills.

Mum actually found her own system for keeping herself on track during the day. I bought her one of the long thin yearly calendars that are made to hang on the wall with a month to a page and the weeks marked clearly. She had a system of crossing through it at certain points in the day. First part of the cross through was made by her at breakfast time, then the second section of the cross would be made by her at lunch time, tea time for the third part of the cross, and then before she went to bed at night she would do the fourth part of the crossing out for that day. I would fill out a week's activities at a time for her on this calendar as she was attending several day centres and had regular meetings with friends so needed the prompt to get ready to go out. This system worked really well for her for a number of years and stopped any confusion about whether it was 7.00am in the morning or 7.00pm at the end of the day as she could glance down at her calendar to see how many marks of the crossing out she had made that day.

Everyone is different in terms of what works for them. The goal is helping them to find ways of controlling their environment and feeling confident that they know what is expected of them as perception of time is something that can get distorted in those suffering from dementia. Strangely enough there was quite a long period when mum couldn't tell the time from clocks or her watch any

The carers often rush around doing things for mum - quickly pulling up her pants, manipulating her arms to get her jumper and cardigan on. Letting her use the commode rather than encouraging her to walk through to the downstairs toilet so she gets to exercise her legs and can wash her hands afterwards. Time for them is at a premium and they often have a long list of clients to visit. I understand. Making her do things for herself keeps her arm and leg muscles toned and strong ... but takes time and patience. This is not something they feel able to do for her. I understand.

I always notice the amazed look on their faces when they find mum stood up manoeuvring the step into the conservatory without help from me, or dressed up ready to go out for lunch. Yes; given time and encouragement she *can* still do things herself.

In hospital three years ago mum was given a plastic "toddler style" drinking cup ... I kept trying to get them to trust her with a mug, however staff were adamant she couldn't use one any more. She was given a spoon not a knife and fork ... Too frail and uncoordinated to use them I was told. Mum likes the feel of a china mug and can use her cutlery properly, so as soon as she was home again she learned to manage with a little encouragement. She is very passive and will happily let anyone take over tasks. She never questions it and without encouragement from me she can easily slip into passive acceptance.

more. However months went by and gradually she seemed to start being able to understand how to tell the time again. I wonder if this is because she had been stressed, and once she was able to relax this ability returned.

Photographs

I've always been a keen photographer like my father; however mum was never that interested and wasn't one for having framed family pictures around her house. However when she started to lose her memory I gathered together quite a few snaps of her favourite sisters. I put them in prominent positions and they seemed to give her a lot of comfort, in particular a head and shoulders one of me that I put in a frame right in front of her chair. I also propped up my self-portrait pencil sketch in her kitchen too. I think psychologically she felt I was there with her all the time as we joked that I was keeping an eye on the carers for her!

Making a "life story book" from photographs

When I was a social worker in the 1980s and 90s I regularly worked with children preparing for a move to an adoptive family. Part of my role was to help them make what we called a "life story book": a scrap book type album filled with photos, cuttings and information about their natural family; foster families they had lived with and important friends. Sometimes even a photo of me was stuck in there too if they wanted one. It is considered a very important document that was vital to a child's sense of wellbeing and their understanding of who they are.

Life story work can be a really useful thing to do with someone with dementia; an illness where so often the person loses their sense of who they are and become very puzzled about their relationship to others around them. You can make it an enjoyable activity that helps to stimulate their memory about their past life, significant people and experiences.

My mum's long term memory was not particularly bad; however I sorted through photo albums and made up small A5 sized books that she could have by her chair to look through. Periodically we had sessions together going through old photographs from her life as a child and young adult. It was a very good trigger for stimulating conversations and brightening her up; and it was interesting for me too. I can hear you say that it sounds very time consuming, but believe me it is valuable as a trigger in leading them down memory lane to a past life and positive thoughts. You might have to persevere at first because they possibly will not recognise people in the photographs; even themselves ... this happened with mum; but with prompting the recognition seemed to come back. I believe that you need to try and be *positive* about the ability of the brain to re-work pathways of understanding and processing information, interpreting things and learning new things too.

Whatever turns you on ...

In an effort to try to stimulate a sufferer's brain you have to search for suitable triggers unique to them. Think back to hobbies and interests they had earlier in their lives and you might find something that stimulates them and gives them enjoyment.

Mum came from Yorkshire and her father was a vet. She would have loved to have followed him into that profession but didn't have the formal education required. It isn't a massive step to see that the James Herriot books of life as a vet in The Dales would be something she would love to read. Mum didn't read them straight through from beginning to end. She was past that stage. However she loved dipping in to the text here and there and that gave her pleasure.

A few years ago when mum was in hospital I found myself really upset at the way she was given a plastic feeder cup when she was perfectly able to hold an ordinary mug or cup. It took me a while to get her back to using ordinary cups on her return home; but it was worth it as she likes using nice china.

Inevitably with her deterioration in the last few weeks she has had a few "accidents", so for safety I have bought her a plastic toddler's feeder cup ... a nice two tone Fuchsia pink one, but I still think she will be offended and I was nervous about showing her for the first time. I needn't have worried as she took one look and exclaimed "Oh I like that; what a lovely colour and it's got handles on both sides. Thank you dear" ... phew; result ... she loves it!

*pink plastic
toddler's feeder cup
with handles on
both sides*

Music, singing and poetry

It has been well documented that singing can be a wonderful way to engage dementia sufferers in something that can stimulate their brain. I love singing and listen to music, so I'm pretty sure *I* will always find it pleasurable. This however is an example of how everyone is different as mum simply *HATED music and singing!* Before she became too frail mum used to go to various day centres twice a week and was always annoyed when it was presumed that she wanted to join in if the group was singing songs. I would have tales of "sing alongs" led by staff that drove her wild as she couldn't get away and the occasional visit from school choirs serenading them with what was in her opinion a torturous din.

She had *always* been like this and when I was a child she would shut me up if I started to sing or had my radio or record player on "too loud" ... so as I've said before *one size doesn't fit all* and it is patronising to the elderly to assume this and lump them all together. Of course there are always silver linings in life if you look hard enough for the positives ... mum became *very* deaf and I could have played heavy rock music right by her head and she would continue smiling.

Daffodils by William Wordsworth 1804

I wander'd lonely as a cloud
That floats on high o'er vales and hills,
When all at once I saw a crowd,
A host of golden daffodils,
Beside the lake, beneath the trees
Fluttering and dancing in the breeze.

Continuous as the stars that shine
And twinkle on the milky way,
They stretch'd in never-ending line
Along the margin of a bay:
Ten thousand saw I at a glance
Tossing their heads in sprightly dance.

Mum may not have liked songs but to my surprise she started to try to recite Wordsworth's poem about daffodils. She kept getting frustrated as she couldn't remember the words. We had been talking that day about the daffodil bulbs I had planted outside her window, and this clearly prompted her to think of this poem from her childhood. I wrote it out for her on a piece of card and she kept it by her seat so she could read it when she wanted. This clearly gave her pleasure and brought tears to her eyes – up to that time I had never heard her recite any poetry; so old memories deep in her brain could be recalled even when she couldn't remember what she had done 5 minutes before. I found that reading this poem over and over again helped mum unlock memories of her happy childhood and prompted some good conversations between us.

Chapter 7

Having a final fling ...

there's hope for all of us if you can flirt and
have fun in your 90's ... .

Having a final fling
... and why not!

My mum had always been a big flirt. I suppose what this really means is she had charm, a warm personality and always made people feel good about themselves. I was used to this aspect of her behaviour. What shocked me was the way that suffering from dementia seemed to cause her to become very much more uninhibited with the opposite sex. It was just as if she was determined to have a final fling; and why not!

What a minx she can be!   *diary entry 2012*

When you retire in your mid-fifties by the time you are in your nineties your savings might be quite depleted ... or even all gone as in my mum's case. Without any funds behind you it can be a nightmare if something in the home breaks down and needs replacing.

When I was a Social Worker in the 1980s I used to apply to charities for families with money problems; never dreaming that one day I would be going that route for my own dear mum ... but needs must. Unfortunately I didn't have savings either to help her out; so when her washing machine needed replacing and her television broke down they were problems I wasn't sure how to deal with. Luckily a good friend prompted me to go down the route of applying to a charity on mum's behalf for assistance ... I was very grateful for this advice as I just hadn't thought of doing this.

Each time an old chap came around to mum's house from the charity to fill in their form and do the necessary paperwork with us. As she is quite deaf I had sat him close to her at the dining table that has a deep fringed cloth on the top. What I hadn't realised was that my demure old mum was squeezing his thigh in a "friendly way" under this table whilst I was busying myself making tea etc. She told me about her actions in a mischievous way a long time after these visits, saying that she had done it to give him a bit of "encouragement"! ... Was this her imagination or did that fringed cloth really cover up a bit of " hankie pankie" between them ... if I'd known I would have been deeply embarrassed as mum would never have done something like that before her dementia. If it was true I just hope he enjoyed the attention ... what a minx!

A few years ago when mum attended a day unit for dementia sufferers at her local hospital she was delighted to tell me that lots of the attendees were men; and a lot of them quite a bit younger than her. She clearly enjoyed herself there and I noticed how close she sat to some of them and there were occasional kisses and holding hands. No one's hubby was safe! Some of the staff there were male and young; so of course they were mum's favourites and when she was discharged she was quite down about it ... but that didn't last long.

The hospital had referred mum to a day centre run by Age Concern. She was in her element there as again quite a few of the attendees were chaps and several times when I popped in I would find her sat on someone's knee, giggling like a school girl, holding hands and doing some outright hard flirting ... Once I'd got over the shock I thought it was really quite positive as she was determined to have fun while she could.

One of the funniest incidents happened when mum was on a ward recuperating from a hip operation. I was visiting her when she started to tell me about the developing relationship she was having with the person in the next bed. When I looked across there was an elderly woman smiling at me. She had a short haircut and a lot of wispy facial hair that resembled a moustache and beard but as it was an all-female ward I *knew* she was *definitely* a woman. Yet mum was adamant this was not the case as they had been flirting together and she was really fond of *him*. Rather sweet. When this lady was discharged a month or so before mum I had to deal with her broken heart!

Chapter 8

Get organised – a recipe for survival

making time for yourself is not something to feel guilty about ...

Get organised – a recipe for survival

Paperwork needs sorting

Once you realise the responsibilities you are facing as a carer you need to get organised concerning paperwork. Being able to *immediately* find the relevant paperwork for something will have a positive impact on your health; you will be less stressed if you have been methodical and created a proper system of storage in *one specially dedicated place* from when you first take over.

The amount of forms, invoices letters and reports that become your responsibility is not to be underestimated. Making space for this paperwork and keeping it filed away conveniently is important for your sanity. I initially made a bit of space in a box file ... then several folders in a drawer. I suggest you have separate folders for hospital and medical, day care invoices, local resources and groups, social services reports, care alarm invoices, household bills, bank statements, will and important documents. You will find these categories grow over the years ... In the last decade mum's paperwork has been breeding in there, helped along by chunky hospital and social services reports, so she had a two drawer filing cabinet in my house all to herself!

Start as you mean to go on and get some labels, clear slings and folders so you can keep relevant things together.

It goes without saying, but I will still remind you that consulting a solicitor and making a Lasting Power of Attorney (LPA) is something we should all do well before we think we might need it so it is there ready to utilise if needed. If the person you are caring for could still be considered in sound mind and they haven't already done this it may not be too late, so look into doing this. It means you can pay bills, operate bank and building society accounts, deal with tax affairs and sort out insurance and repairs on the person's behalf if they become mentally incapacitated.

The second type of LPA is concerned with health and welfare and, in particular, the following aspects, but only when the person is unable to act for himself or herself: It relates to decisions regarding treatment and care: where the person should live and with whom; who may visit and who is excluded; arranging holidays and outings; making end-of-life decisions. You should discuss with a solicitor whether you need both forms or not as it depends on everyone's individual circumstances ... but the financial one is a must.

Also if it is not too late and they could still be considered of sound mind, you could suggest they *make a will*. So many people mean to get around to these two things, but leave it too late. Certainly don't let the cost of making this and the Power of Attorney put you off as not having them in place can be a very expensive business.

Staying calm to survive

I often had to just walk away to another room to calm myself down when I started to feel the adrenaline pumping around my system when dealing with mum. Little "accidents" that meant I ended up on my arthritic knees cleaning something off the floor or explaining something to her for the umpteenth time through gritted teeth because she immediately forgot. Yes, at these times I could feel my heart beat racing and I was usually having a menopausal flush too. Double whammy. It was really fun being a middle-aged carer!

I increasingly found that it was easier to call her "dear" or "darling" on these occasions. Maybe this was a way I could distance myself from the situation as I could do the jobs in a loving way but she was becoming less and less like my "mum" … a title that has so many strong emotional feelings related to it.

Ideally if I was feeling stressed when I left the room I should have settled down somewhere and done some deep breathing and meditation focusing on a peaceful place from my imagination … hah; good idea; maybe I'll try that in another life!

A bit of bread with her butter …   *diary entry March 2015*

I took some home-made bread over to mum this afternoon for her to try. I buttered it and although she said it was delicious she was just scraping the butter off with her teeth and leaving the bread. Maybe she would like a bit more butter and a little jam on it I thought. Yes, she would, came the reply: however the same scenario of scrapping off the topping with her teeth … and leaving the bread. After the third go I had to leave the room to calm down as it was an insult to my baking … no, I'm joking. I just wanted to put the kettle on again.

It isn't funny really; I think she finds swallowing more difficult these days. You just have to be patient and flexible with what you give her to eat. Give mum sweets, chocolate, cakes and buttered chips. All these slide down beautifully!

As mum deteriorated it got easier in some ways to accept the role of carer. The sense of acceptance helps you become more calm … you spend months even years going round and round in circles trying to find a scenario that releases you … but eventually you come to the conclusion that *acceptance* of the situation is the only way to survive.

Making a break for it

Of course there were times when that calm serenity was challenged. Friends chat on about holidays they are taking to exciting places, seemingly unaware of my yearning to travel and feel the sand between my toes again. I would have *loved* to have holidays too but:

a) I couldn't afford one.
b) Mum's care whilst I was away would have been prohibitively expensive.
c) I reckoned the fallout from going away would have meant lots of extra work on my return and deterioration in mum's condition as a consequence.
d) I don't think I could have enjoyed a minute of my time away as I would have been worrying about what was happening to her.

It was years without a "proper" holiday. In that time I had two overnight stays away from home that were fantastic and a couple of nights staying with a friend. However mum managed to have an "emergency" during that longer break. She had dropped the front door catch on the carers so a drama ensued that nearly involved the local police breaking her door down to get access, so I ended up sat on my friend's sofa sobbing my eyes out that evening … it was sorted, but not before I had been "punished" for going away!

I found it was far better to have regular outings with friends at a distance that is near enough for you to respond to an emergency at home. Less worry, a refreshing change of scenery and a chance to talk, exchange ideas and recharge your batteries. No point in yearning after what you can't have … it leads to insanity

> ## Just make sure that you give yourself **regular breaks**, even if they are only for a few hours, so you avoid having a **"breakdown"**

Find time to be completely selfish

If you neglect yourself you cannot be an effective carer. You *must* make sure you have time for relaxation and pleasure. The ideal situation is to have plenty of other support around you taking some of the pressure of the day to day care. This then makes it so much easier for you to engage in a positive way with the person you are looking after as you will be less worn down. *You're not being selfish at all as it is a win- win situation* as, if you are refreshed, you will be a better carer and less up tight or resentful.

Making time for yourself is not something to feel guilty about. Keep reminding yourself of this!

After an outing to meet a friend for coffee or an hour or two out of the house following a hobby your batteries will be re-charged and you will feel better. The trouble is that even with large families it seems that usually one individual takes on the role of main carer. In my case all my relatives live in other parts of the country, so it has been friends who have had the job of keeping me going. If you don't feel supported enough and friends and family seem to "slide away", you need to try and engage with groups or organisations who can offer you help.

"Poo pie" film   **diary entry New Year's Day 2014**

Whilst chatting to a friend on the phone about what was on TV last night we both decided to watch "The Help"; an Oscar winning drama from the point of view of African-American housemaids working for white families in a southern state. It was about the hardships they went through and their struggle against mistreatment.

When we texted each other the following day we both agreed it had been a good film. I told her that my favourite bit had been when one of the maids put her own excrement inside the ingredients of a Mississippi mud pie she gave as a gift to a woman she had worked for who had been cruel to her. What an act of revenge!

My friend texted back to me: "Now don't go getting ideas!" – referring to the "Poogate" episode on Christmas Day. The immediate thought that went through my head; repulsing me at the same time as I was laughing at the craziness of it was that in my case it was far more likely that I had inadvertently eaten something tainted with mum's poo in her house over the last few years … it just doesn't bear thinking about!!!

You might be someone who still has all the thoughts and feelings we have been discussing in this book despite the fact that the person you are caring for is in residential care and not with you. It could seem like everyone expects you to be relieved and ready to get on with your life as you aren't doing the day to day tasks of looking after them. What is often not acknowledged is that this can be a time of terrible loss and change when you might be feeling awful with little control over what is happening to them. You might be suffering the constant worry of whether the home is caring for them properly.

It needs to be acknowledged that whilst they are on this planet and vulnerable because of their illness you could quite possibly be feeing under pressure of one sort or another.

Support from the heavens

Help comes from unexpected places and often from people you hadn't really thought of turning to for support. Mum had a super neighbour who was nearly 40 years younger than her, but despite this age gap they had a nice relationship for many years. They used to occasionally socialise over coffee or a glass of wine in each other's houses; that sort of thing. She could be thought of as someone who has enough to do without involving herself in mum's care as she worked and had a family; however she always made time for mum. When mum became ill she was a great help: waiting for ambulances, visiting mum in hospital, putting out mum's dustbins each week, holding mum's key and dealing with the times when the carer's had problems with the key safe or gaining access. Her help was invaluable as I live six miles away and she was a few doors down from mum. Help that is much appreciated and certainly was not expected … *and* she was always there for me to have a moan to as she looked after some of her own relatives and appreciated what I was going through. Lucky me!

The little girl who used to climb through the privet hedge running between the neighbours garden to spend time with mum is now a pensioner herself. (She is one of those ageless arty types with bright red hair cut in a short bob, zany glasses and stylish clothing with a very young attitude) She has actually been amazingly helpful to me and very caring towards mum. She had relatives in her partner's family with similar problems so she had practical experiences and advice she was able to share with me. Over the years she has always been happy to talk about "feelings" on the phone when I desperately needed a chat to cheer me up and, because she was so fond of mum, it meant a great deal to have her support as I knew she really cared on a deep level. A regular phone call was a real lifeline and helped counteract the feelings of isolation I suffered.

She also pointed me in the direction of my local Alzheimer's Society when mum was initially diagnosed. They were fantastic. I first called in at their centre when I was reeling at the shock of mum having a diagnosis of vascular dementia. I sat going through their box of tissues and getting lots of tea, sympathy and most of all lots of practical advice about what I need to do. In that first year I attended support groups on relevant topics, went to talks and had several free reflexology sessions that made me feel great and were excellent therapy ... just what I needed at the time as I was so stressed.

The main thing is to make sure you don't suffer alone in silence, not talking to anyone about your situation and how you feel. Bottling things up will only harm you. Talking about what you are experiencing is *not disloyal* to the person you are caring for; it is *essential* to your mental health! There are forums and blogs for carers on the internet and local support groups you can join, just make sure you get socialising somehow and make a positive change to your life.

My escape to another world ...

Local libraries

I have always loved libraries. A local library is a fantastic resource with books on every subject from A–Z. Being a carer often means you are poor in the finances area; however with a trip to the library every few weeks you can stock up on £100s worth of literature without money changing hands ... great! You can take home books that help you in your caring role, books on adventure, travel, romance. Pure escapism is a wonderful experience and will take you to a different place in your mind and relax your thoughts.

I have been a member of a book club for years now. We started the group after the evening of my "divorce party" where a few of my friends who were also old colleagues from work expressed an interest in getting together more often as we never seemed to find the time to see each other regularly in our busy lives. Some friends of friends joined in over the years and now there are 10 of us meeting in each other's houses on a rota basis. With a meeting each month we get through quite a lot of books and the discussions can be very stimulating when we are on form and the book chosen has been a meaty one. I did drop out for about three years whilst mum was staying with me as I couldn't leave her in my house on her own ... she just wouldn't let me. On the page opposite is a list of our top reads just in case you need some inspiration to a) start reading more or even better b) start a book club yourself.

Some of our favourite books from my reading group:

"The Kite Runner"	Khaled Hosseini
"The Rosie Project"	Graeme Simsion
"The Minaturist"	Jessie Burton
"Suite Francaise"	Irene Nemirosky
"The Secret Life of Bees"	Sue Monk Kidd
"One Good Turn"	Kate Atkinson
"Case Histories"	Kate Atkinson
"Theodora – Actress, Empress, Whore"	Stella Duffy
"Winter in Madrid"	C J Sansom
"The Cuckoo Calling"	Robert Galbraith
"The Silkworm"	Robert Galbraith

Chapter 9

Keeping healthy as a carer

you need to keep fit … it's a tough job!

Keeping healthy as a carer

Eating well – fresh food versus processed

As a carer your diet will need to be extra-nutritious to combat the stress you are under, and how can you manage if you fall ill? There is a saying from China that "disaster enters through the mouth"; so best keep your mouth shut … no just joking. What they mean is take care you eat food that suits *your* body and is good for *your* health. We are all different in the way our digestion works, but if you come up with a diet plan that crisps and takeaways suit you, try again! Eating a good nutritious diet was sometimes difficult in my situation as I constantly found myself trying to coax mum to eat something by eating the same thing myself to encourage her. Her favourite foods were pork pies, sausages, ham sandwiches, sweets and cream cakes … . I would usually try and avoid such things for health reasons, but in an effort to get her to swallow something … *anything* … I've been known to eat *my* plate full *and* all the leftovers in frustration … just like looking after a young child!

If you are anything like me you will be constantly worrying that you might suffer from dementia at some stage later in your life. Every week in the press there is another report of what we should or shouldn't do to avoid this nasty disease. It is all very confusing as we are so bombarded with advice it is difficult to work out what might be worth following in terms of diet and lifestyle choices. In some instances it seems to be our genetic inheritance that can predispose us to suffering certain types of dementia which is frightening for those families affected. On a more optimistic note however it seems that for most of us research is indicating that there are things we might be able to do ourselves to try and avoid getting this disease. Learning a second language and keeping the brain actively learning new things seems to pay dividends in later life. For me personally there are a few things that I have taken on board from my reading around the subject that I think might help me to avoid getting dementia in the future, but of course only time will tell …

I have to hold up my hand to being a bit obsessed with food and admit to being a highly neurotic, health food, knit your own yoghurt type of person. Every faddy diet or new superfood mentioned in the media has my immediate attention. I believe in the wisdom of the old Chinese saying "Let food be your medicine" … and I have *always* been like this. I am told that even as a toddler I was asking the adults "Is this good for me?" when they presented me with a something to eat. Yes; a weird picky eater who peeled the pastry away and just nibbled at the filling of pies and would carefully peel batter off her fish and discard it … .However I was the usual human muddle of contradictions. I had a love of chocolate and unfortunately there was a 3 mile walk to school and 3 miles back each day; passing several paper shops selling confectionary, so I always pigged out on sweets prior to mealtimes ... and then didn't want to eat my meal. As I grew up I reckon my brain's main food was SUGAR, and scientists who are looking into what causes dementia and a whole lot of other diseases seem to think that is a very bad thing ... Oh dear!

In the 1960s when I was a child there was a new era of processed food coming on to the market that seemed so exciting to everyone. Luckily mum was a great cook, so we still had a reasonable balance of good quality meals that were cooked from fresh ingredients, but as a working mother she was also happy to save time by giving us instant mashed potato, butterscotch whip out of a packet for pudding, full of chemicals and nasties, or a powdery packet curry as a treat. We had never tasted anything like it. Flavourings and preservatives tasted amazing! Looking back it was really funny that I would be sat on the sofa scoffing sweets and biscuits ... whilst reading mum's copy of "Here's Health". This magazine became a regular in our house for years as mum became more interested in the importance of good nutrition through her Yoga. We followed their advice of eating wholemeal bread instead of white, and from butter to cold-pressed margarine. I can recall vividly how I absolutely hated the nasty dark bread that tasted so bitter and had a funny dense texture. It just shows how what we like to eat is a matter of habit, as it didn't take long before I was converted.

What an appetite for sauciness!   *diary entry December 2012*

I took mum for lunch today and she ordered sausage and chips. 3 really large Cumberland sausages arrived on her plate. Clearly they were just too much for her to eat so I asked the waitress to pop the last one in a doggy bag as I thought a nice sausage sandwich for her tea was a good idea.

The waitress said they had stopped doing cardboard "doggy bags" but she would be happy to wrap the one not eaten in cling film for mum. When she came back to our table with the pink coloured sausage wrapped in plastic mum looked up delighted. She took it in her hand and waved it in the air suggestively saying: "Ooh lovely ... I'm going to have a lot of fun with this tonight!" Needless to say there were quite a few startled faces amongst the other diners nearby and some laughter too: particularly the waitress who has known mum for years.

I can also remember when yoghurt first arrived in the supermarkets. None of the brands had live cultures in and all of it was packed full of sugar along with lots of jammy like fruit ... apart from calories and a bit of calcium I reckon it did more harm than good but was a real hit with the public ... I adored it and ate at least one pot a day thinking I was doing wonders for my health. ... just shows how I believed the adverts that showed young fit skiers jumping around full of energy. A big dose of scepticism is always a good way to look at any articles or adverts about food ... and before you ask, yes, for many years now I have made my own yoghurt! For me this is particularly important when making yoghurt out of organic soya milk as I don't want any of the additives usually added to the brands available in the supermarket.

Mum on the other hand grew up on a farm in the middle of the Yorkshire Dales fed on good wholesome plain fresh food with no tuck shops in her area. A small bag of sweets was a rare treat. She went to boarding school in term time where again the food was uninspiring, plain and freshly cooked as there was no alternative in the 1930s – 40s. She had memories of climbing plum trees in the orchards of the farm and sitting up in the branches gorging on ripe fruit, and helping herself in the well-stocked larder of the farmhouse kitchen full of delicious food when feeling peckish. It was certainly a healthy start whatever happened to her later on in life!

It really is a wonder that I'm not massively fat as turning to food for comfort is so natural to me. I am greedy by nature and over the years my weight has gone up and down like most women. Food is my preferred drug; especially chocolate! When the stress of being mum's carer got to me this is what I turned to ... If I smoked I would have been on 40 a day and if I had been a drinker I could easily have hit the bottle. Everyone *needs* relaxation and pleasure; but it is often a struggle to try and make sure it is something that doesn't have a negative impact on health. What I have realised is that if I avoid processed food, in particular cakes and sweets, I tend to feel slimmer and healthier ... .and better able to bend down clean up spills, fasten shoes and lift someone on to a commode ... Lucky me!

Things I try to avoid

The first big "baddie" I can point the finger at is SUGAR. (Including honey and dried fruits too) It has been suggested that it ages our brains. As someone with a very sweet tooth and lots of dental decay to prove it, this is horrifying to hear. I type this as I'm sitting in my office eating chocolate ... there is no hope for me as I'm severely addicted.

As I have been conscious of being a sugar addict all my life , in recent years I have worked quite hard on reducing my consumption by using Stevia as a sugar substitute in drinks , sauces and baking. Initially this was by growing the actual Stevia plant in our greenhouse and then chopping it up and storing it dried in a jar. That meant funny green flecks in everything; and although it made things sweet it *looked* awful.

Luckily I had a friend who ran a website selling natural products. She used to supply me with it from Canada in the form of white powder in clear plastic bags before it was readily available here in the UK. That used to make me smile as it meant I had a tin in the cupboard that was full of small packets that resembled a stash of cocaine. Now I can just buy this natural product in the form of pure white powder from a local health shop (avoid the brands with fillers and other ingredients from supermarkets) ... it is a case of experimenting when using it in cooking as it only takes a teeny tiny pinch to add sweetness, so you have to be careful not to overdo it.

It has also been suggested that COFFEE is bad with TEA only marginally less detrimental to your brain. Coffee gives me palpitations so I can't drink it anyway, but *I love* my cups of tea. I've tried to do without them but failed.

FATTY and PROCESSED meat is bad too. You must avoid clogging up the arteries to the brain. GOOD FATS are essential to the brain; so whilst you might need to ease up on eating too many pork pies and sausages you need to eat *more* fish, eggs, nuts and seeds for the omegas ... ... and don't fry food; poach, boil or steam so you don't create nasty damaging trans fats.

"Fancy a jacket or new potatoes with your meal mum?" Why do I bother asking as I know the answer I am going to get ...

"Oooh, chips please!"

Even the chips clearly aren't greasy enough for mum now. We were eating our pub lunch today when I left the table for a minute to go to the toilet. I saw mum lean over to my plate and pinch my two individually wrapped portions of butter that were for my jacket potato. She didn't think I was watching her as she opened them up and slathered butter on her chips one at a time and popped them in her mouth. Not a pretty sight for the other diners!

ALCOHOL is a big problem as it causes damage to brain cells every time we drink it. I don't want to ruin everyone's fun, so best just to try and be moderate and always take it with plenty of water to mitigate the dehydration factor.

SMOKING is another thing that possibly accounts for decreased circulation to the brain in dementia sufferers. So if you are one of the minority of smokers still puffing away in your back garden or on the pavement outside offices, shops and restaurant this might persuade you to think about stopping. My mother did actually stop smoking at the ripe old age of 71; having smoked since she was a child of 8. Apparently she used to pinch the tab ends discarded by the farm hands or take a few cigarettes at a time from the large box her mother had on their sofa table. At 71 her chest was a noisy rattling bag of wheeziness; however within a year or two of giving up her breathing was far better and she could walk farther ... so it is never too late, but I reckon without the ciggies mum might have lived to 100 easily. That is a strange thought for someone who was a reluctant carer!

What I include in my diet

Now for the things that are suggested to be positively good for protecting against dementia type deterioration in the brain:

GARLIC and ONIONS are a food that should be eaten daily because of their effect on the flow of blood to the brain. Try and consume some of the garlic raw as it is more potent health wise in that form. You might lose a few friends and your partner could leave you; but it might help keep your arteries free flowing.

Just like all mums tell you "eat up your greens", it turns out that GREEN LEAFY VEGETABLES are an important part of the diet to fight brain deterioration. Also make sure you eat plenty of BLUE and RED COLOURED BERRIES. Increasing the consumption of vegetable protein by eating more PULSES such as peas, broad beans, lentils and chickpeas is also thought to be a good idea.

High doses of B VITAMINS have been suggested as a protective daily supplement, particularly B12 and B6 and B2. The list of things to do or supplements to take grows with each research project. More recently I read somewhere that the spice TURMERIC had a protective effect on the brain … so I rushed out and bought a packet and started adding it to stews and stir fries … quite delicious once you get over the earthy slightly bitter taste. I hadn't specifically used it on its own before, only as an ingredient in ready mixed curry powder as it is quite a strong dye and I am a messy cook; but if it is good for my brain I thought I'll give it a go. The trouble is that now my kitchen tea towels are streaked in orange … You will have guessed that basically I am quite neurotic at the best of times and whatever article on combating dementia I read I absorb the advice and if it makes sense I follow it (apart from anything that suggests I stop eating chocolate or drinking tea … we all have our non-negotiable areas)

The above suggestions have been gleaned by me from reading articles in newspapers and health magazines, and listening to the news. Probably some of the research leaves a lot to be desired and other suggestions will be proved wrong with the passage of time. I haven't gone into any detail as what I tell you here could probably be out of date even before this book is published. However I reckon there *might* be *some truth* in *some* of the research, so I wanted to share it with you. (I just hope they're wrong on chocolate and tea …)

Oh, and before I forget you will need to avoid POLLUTION and STRESS as they might be factors too. I knew there was a catch …

Laughter therapy

Looking after mum for years on end turned me into a bit of a miserable mess as I became so mired in feeling sorry for myself and my situation. I would find myself dreading going to visit her and I would find that my jaw was clenched and my heart was beating fast just before seeing her as I never knew what I would have to face.

One of my friends who had listened patiently many times to my negative outpourings over the phone was getting so fed up she felt I needed to change my attitude. She rang me one day with news of a therapy I had never heard of.

She had been in the audience at a talk about "laughter therapy" and when it was over she went to talk to the speaker as she had found it very interesting. It was one of those strange coincidences in life as my friend was at a conference centre in Manchester and the practitioner actually lived hundreds of miles away ... in the same town as me!

My pal took her telephone number and I rang her straight away to arrange a meeting. We got together in a local cafe and I have to say that I turned out to be a natural actress and could burst into spontaneous laughter at the drop of a hat. Marvellous! I found out that however down I was I could come out with a laugh that became more natural within a few seconds as I loosened up ... This was a revelation to me and quite surprising as I've always been rather shy. I didn't need to join the group as it was a technique I could use straight away ... strangely if I was just about to go into "panic mode" immediately reversing my *physical* state by roaring with laughter seemed to short circuit the messages in my body ... and I felt better!

Laughter really is a mini workout as it is an aerobic activity referred to as "internal jogging" by laughter therapists as all the intercostal muscles get a workout. There have even been studies to show that it lowers blood sugar levels; is good for your heart and circulation and also boosts your infection fighting anti-bodies; whereas stress can deplete your immunity.

There is scientific research to support these claims; so even though you might feel really silly having a go **it *will* work** as it massages the abdomen and releases tension in the solar plexus ... also using the smiling muscles sends feel good endorphins to our brains that make us happy. So despite the circumstances you find yourself in you can create good feelings by smiling or laughing. You probably think that you might need external prompts to get into this new activity such as watching a funny film or your favourite comedian; reading a humorous book or looking through some photos of amusing times in your life ... whilst other people are like me and can get going from a completely "cold start". To do this you just begin by saying "Ha,ha,ha ... " and pull wide the corners of your mouth into a smile ... .go on; have a try! Of course get-togethers with friends often create the best atmosphere for spontaneous laughter; but I am presuming that maybe like me you are stuck in an isolated position as a carer and don't have this luxury ...

There are lots of therapeutic laughter clubs worldwide, with some where you meet up as a group and others on the web using skype or telephone contact ... .there are even Laughter Yoga groups on offer in some areas as it is becoming increasingly popular. I've found it a great help in raising my mood and making me better able to cope. If you want to give it a try start upturning the corners of your mouth rather than setting your jaw into the "carer's scowl" and have a go at laughing at nothing in particular. It is easier than you think. Honestly ... try it a few times and it should work for you too. ... it is a case of not caring whether people around you think you are mad ... so what if they do! Lose your inhibitions and have a go. I have been known to laugh in shops, walking down the road, driving along in my car or sat in a café; so if you see a woman alone laughing, it might be me and you will know that I'm counteracting some dark thoughts about life ...

Yoga

When introducing you to my mum's earlier life I told you about her teaching Yoga. I firmly believe it is a wonderful discipline and incredibly powerful in helping the body to move well and remain healthy. It is also fantastic for calming the mind through control of the breathing during exercises. I was a member of my local health club for years and regularly joined in with the Yoga sessions 3 - 4 times a week. However in recent years the fees seemed a bit steep so I have been practising on my own at home in front of the bedroom mirror ... much cheaper, but requiring a lot more will power as no one there to make you do the positions you find difficult; so I always end up just doing my favourites that I can perform easily. This is not a good idea really as you need the guidance of a teacher.

I even practise some postures during the course of the day. When I am in a queue at the supermarket or stood peeling vegetables in the kitchen I will stand on one leg for a while; then the other in "Tree Pose" as improving balance is apparently important for the brain. I often exercise my arms by doing prayer position with arms behind my shoulders if I've been on the computer or sat too long ... weaving poses into your daily jobs is an idea but be *very careful* as you don't want to end up in hospital! ... and also never go into corpse position at the end of a session without making sure there are no practical jokers in the room as I've still got my neck injury from mum's playful little scrunch to my face!

Buddhism

Using my local library I read around the subject of Buddhist philosophy a few years ago at a time when mum had a long stay in hospital. This was so helpful in changing my attitude to the caring role. I started to see I was just being *too emotional* to be effective. A lot of the books on Buddhism were difficult to understand; but I found an absolute gem in "How to Become a Buddha in 5 Weeks – the simple way to self-realisation" by Giulio Cesare Giacobbe. This book is a very slim volume that is easy to read. I highly recommend it to anyone

Mum aged 85 doing a yoga shoulder stand in a
hotel bedroom – instant facelift without surgery

searching for help as the author had suffered the death of his young son, yet is able to help others with his wisdom and advice.

My feelings were really all about *me* and "losing" a loving parent ... who was still here on planet earth; but not the same person. Yes; I felt really sorry for myself! I needed to detach myself from her and be a little more dispassionate about the loss I was suffering as the essence of her character as a person I loved ebbed away. The whole process was very much like bereavement ... but you just don't know when the funeral will be! Doctors had told me it was a matter of months and at the time I wasn't sure she would pull through ... well mum lived on for another 3 years.

> # My attachment to her was painful. Once I decided to look upon my caring role more as **a job of work** it became much easier

Mum came out of hospital and my new philosophy of taking each and every day as it came without jumping ahead in my mind allowed me to **focus on making her comfortable and happy *now; today*.** Tomorrow maybe things will change or other plans will need to be discussed. Accepting that life is precarious and no one can predict or control the future helped me to relax in to the caring role. I learned not to run ahead in my imagination regarding what *might* happen in the future as negative thoughts can be so destructive. I just tried to live for the moment, making the most of what I had whilst doing the caring tasks to the best of my ability.

In the west we tend to live life like a race for acquiring "things" such as status, money and possessions. Why are we never satisfied? Buddhism teaches us that all we really have is the present of the moment we are in ... that is our reality, so we need to *treasure each moment*. If we are eating an apple let's sit down and savour every juicy bite and marvel at the beautiful colour of the rosy skin. If we are watching our favourite programme on TV we should say a silent thank you for our ability to experience such a fabulous invention not available to previous generations. A walk outside, even in the rain can be a great pleasure if we breathe in the fresh air and remind ourselves how thankful we should be, as in other parts of the world this might be prohibited to females or even a dangerous

Katie joining in
with exercises

thing to do for either sex. Remind yourself to be grateful for the nice things in your life. It is a good idea to get a piece of paper and make a list.

If you are so down you can't think of much then that should definitely persuade you to 1) Visit your GP and 2) *change your attitude*! If you are feeling angry and resentful at your situation as a carer you are going to miss out on all the amazing positive things in your life ... many of them free of charge!

The present is all any of us have got. Being serene and calm and dealing with all that the day gives us in a good humour doesn't depend on the situation we are living in; but on our *reaction* to what happens. I am constantly reminding myself of this. It is just like having two voices in your head and once you recognise a negative thought you can challenge it and counteract it with a positive slant ... then give yourself a big smile as you are beginning to re-programme your mind. Just keep practising!

The thought process of our minds can be manipulated and trained with practice. You need to recognise any patterns in your thoughts towards "negative thinking" and realise that once you can label them as such their power will diminish ... and the *fear* that fills you when you think like that will go too.

Practise "positive thinking" and it will make you a stronger person and a far better carer. You can create mantras that you speak out loud to yourself to give you strength. So you don't get strange looks it is probably best to use these when you are alone. I have developed the habit of giving myself the following pep talk in front of my bedroom mirror:

"I am calm and relaxed. *Nothing* bothers me.
I am strong and healthy.
I am glad to be alive"

... and all the time I am giving myself a big smile ... I might even throw in a bit of spontaneous laughter ...

"she's losing it" I hear you say ...

Take a bit of thought to work out your own personal mantra ... a few words that will reinforce your thoughts with strength and good energy. This can be a very powerful tool as your brain is always listening to what comes out of your mouth ... and it tends to believe what it hears!

Get moving- walking your way to health

OK, so you feel sorry for yourself. You are trapped in a prison and the only form of comfort is the biscuit tin ... *don't do it.* Put those custard creams down; you'll go and eat the whole packet if you sit on the sofa with them! It is so tempting to scoff your way to oblivion. However lifting someone off the toilet or bending down to Velcro their shoes for them is much harder to do if you've got a fat tummy in the way. Far more likely to slip a disc or give yourself a hernia.

It is blowing a gale and raining so you sit slothfully in a chair eating those custard creams. Yes; a walk in the fresh air is preferable, but your excuse is you don't want to get wet/cold/blown on by the fierce wind. *Don't do this to yourself* ... you have to stay fit to be a carer.

If you can afford it you can go to a local gym session; but even better is to start exercise sessions in your own house. The benefit is that there is no payment or fee, you can wear what you have on already, do it at *any time* and in *any room* and for *just as long* as you want. *Perfect!* Mum loved me to have a little dance in front of her ... she usually started laughing at me, so that was a result as it did her good and me too!

Suggestions for easy exercises at home

- Jog on the spot for a few minutes

- Walk up and down the first few steps of the staircase until you get puffed

- Turn on the radio and have a dance to a few tracks

- Jump on the spot or use a skipping rope (mind the chandelier)

Some of the best advice I received was from friends who kept *on* and *on* about how I needed to get walking outside *every day, preferably in the mornings*. They were worried that I wasn't getting enough exercise and I was becoming unfit. I had been a member of a gym for years but had to give it up because it was too expensive. Just at a crucial time when I needed my strength more than ever I felt I couldn't afford to exercise. They made me see that was a crazy way of thinking. Generally apart from wearing out your shoes, walking doesn't cost anything and does wonders for your mood, metabolism and peps up all your bodily functions. If you could patent it and put it in a drug you'd make a fortune as it works brilliantly!

Walking is therapeutic and you can double the impact on your life by walking somewhere that might save you money now you are quite probably in a pickle financially. Even if you are not it can be healthy fun … which brings me on to how useful car boots can be to carers …

The need for a hobby - "car boot" therapy

Going to car boots is my hobby. I just love them. Whatever it is that you enjoy doing; be it basket weaving or playing golf, you need to find a way of keeping it in your life. It is all too easy to slip into a situation where you end up doing nothing pleasurable for yourself when you are drawn in to the caring role. If you already have a hobby, cherish it and don't give it up. If you don't have a hobby think of what you might do to give yourself some pleasurable times away from your caring role … you deserve it.

I used to go to car boots regularly even when I was well off with no real financial incentive as I am a magpie who loves collecting old things and I also can't resist a bargain. You could even call it an addiction of mine. It is a win-win situation, as whilst you are wandering around the stalls sifting through the 99% dross, you often see something you need at a bargain price. I have been a car boot fan since they began decades ago; before that I was a keen attendee at jumble sales and a "skip dipper" as I love a good rummage.

Car boots have been brilliant as sources of clothing for mum as with her increased incontinence she needed lots of pairs of pyjamas for a daily change. She became so tiny I had to find them in children's sizes; this was fine as usually they were like new because kids grow out of them so quickly. Also she needed plenty of daywear after losing so much weight. People throw out lovely jumpers and trousers after wearing them just a few times so she had lovely warm polo necks and cardigans; all very good brands and items that would cost a lot if purchased from the shops … and whilst buying them I've usually had some fresh air and lots of exercise … and the thrill of a bargain!

When mum was in her 90s I found that trying to put her earrings in was proving too difficult as her earlobes had become so thin and fragile; I just couldn't find the pierced hole in her ear anymore. Well again car boots came up trumps and I was able to buy her several pairs of lovely vintage clip on earrings that only cost pence, so she continued going out feeling glamourous. Nothing shoddy for her!

Remember to be selfish
as that will keep you going!

Starting my day well

For decades I started my day with a large dose of the Today programme on Radio 4 each morning. Absolutely nothing wrong with that; however as my life took a change of direction,(I won't say downward slide as that would be too negative) I began to find the subjects discussed were things I didn't want to hear when I had just woken up and was getting ready for my caring tasks. I realised that it was rather depressing hearing politicians droning on and presenters talking ad nauseam to bankers and financiers about what a mess the world was in. Don't get me wrong I still *love* Radio 4; just not *first thing*.

I have been thinking a lot about how our brain processes what we listen to. I realised that whilst waking up in the morning it is important to programme my brain for a good and positive day ahead. Over the last few years a big noisy dose

of Radio 2 has done the trick. The presenters are just brilliant and bounce off each other with plenty of spontaneous repartee and always seem to be full of fun and light-hearted banter. I often end up smiling or laughing at what they are talking about as the programmes are so upbeat, but even more important than that is Radio 2 plays lots of music that I can dance to in bed … under the covers! Yes crazy though this may sound it is a great way to stretch my muscles and get a warm up in for my arthritic joints in *before* getting out of bed. I start by removing the pillow from behind my head so I can lie flat … then I get moving! If you've got a partner just warn them before you start as there could be arms flung around and legs kicking to the beat. I am not joking.

I reckon that if you are caring for someone and finding the job hard you need to practise smiling a lot and laughing in order to feel good. Radio 2 helps me start each day well with a bout of singing and a bit of dancing mixed with stretching exercises whilst still in bed. Your idea of hell? … OK; try radio 3 and let your psyche absorb some classical music: or maybe just stretch a little and do a bit of meditation in silence. I just advise not listening too hard to the news and

gloves fixed on elastic pinned to
the inside collar of mum's
jacket and a bum bag rather
than a handbag made going out
much easier!

current affairs first thing in the morning as you brain takes in all that despair and sadness and you set the day off on the wrong note in your thoughts. This is the case for *me*; but maybe you are someone who would take all that news and it will be processed by your brain into a positive feeling of "thank God I wasn't in that plane crash, suffering from that disease or living under that regime" … In that case ignore the last few paragraphs.

Chapter 10

Postscript

happy days are here again ...

Postscript

I had finished the draft for this book and was working on the preliminary sketches when mum died suddenly just three weeks short of her 95th birthday. I never got to read it through to her, but she knew I was working on it. She was a very proud dignified lady, so it is probably for the best, as she might have taken exception to some of the cartoons and descriptions of her behaviour. In retrospect I was very blessed as she slipped away one morning just as the carer was getting her breakfast ready with no warning signs other than her gradually increasing frailty … as apart from her dementia she seemed OK, although she had felt rather cold the previous night. In retrospect however I recall that she had started to say she didn't want to go out for a coffee or for lunch in the preceding weeks; opting for meals prepared at home which was not like her as she loved going out … so maybe she was just gradually fading away. I had been dreading any incident that would lead to mum being hospitalised again as she was so afraid of that

---

They've given me the wrong person!　　　　**diary entry July 15th 2015**

Today I arranged to pick up mum's ashes from the undertakers. A friend offered to come with me and I was very grateful as it is difficult to park by their shop … just as I expected there wasn't a parking space so I had to pull in and make a dash for it whilst she looked out for traffic wardens. In the reception area there were several plastic carrier bags with cardboard boxes inside. I quickly explained I was in a hurry and they passed me one of the bags. I almost collapsed under the weight of it as I staggered out and made towards the car … .My friend saw my difficulty and asked what was wrong … .

I blurted out "They've given me the wrong person; mum was light as a feather; a 6 stone bag of bones and these ashes weigh a ton!" Help, quick, I need to move the car!" I jumped in the driving seat and we sped off giggling at the idea that they had accidentally given us the ashes of some chap weighing 20 stone instead of mum … Once we were away from the high street we parked up somewhere quiet and I opened the boot and read the label … yes, it was her name on the urn. Maybe they had put the big man's ashes in with her by mistake … .more laughter as we both reckoned mum would be looking down and laughing with us at the situation.

I mused for a while about keeping her urn permanently in the boot of my car as there was nothing mum liked more than a trip out; but common sense prevailed …

happening. I therefore feel very glad that she left this world so peacefully whilst she still lived in her own home. After years of devoting my time to her care I had imagined being very sad and feeling rather lost when this finally happened; however the laughter and jokes continued after she died ...

She was my best friend and I must say that perhaps if she had died younger I would have had a bad time grieving for the loss of her in my life. I reckon when dementia affects a loved one you can go through the grieving process well before they actually die over a much longer period of years before their actual demise – I had great sadness and tears over the years as her personality ebbed away and we could no longer have meaningful conversations together. Friends thought I would be very emotional when she actually died because the two of us had been so close. I was shocked, yes, but the main feeling I had was of relief and I'm not ashamed of admitting that.

I consider myself to have been extremely lucky to have had such an inspirational character for a mother. She had a formidable intellect before her decline; yet like many of her generation of females mum didn't get the education and encouragement to make the most of her talents.

I hope that this book will be of help to the current generation of women (and a few men) who might find themselves in a similar predicament to me. Mum had a role as an amateur psychologist for friends and relatives to turn to for advice, so I am sure she would love the idea that her story in this book might prove helpful in opening up what is a difficult subject as it offers solutions to coping without going crazy ... good luck reader; I hope it gives you a few laughs and some useful tips.

Ten Top Tips

1 Ask for Help

Don't be too proud to look for support. Get proactive and search out information on what is available in your area. Routes to this information are through your GP, the social services department at your local council, local groups run by charities such as Age Concern, Crossroads, the Alzheimer's Society or Admiral Nurses. Just make sure you are not struggling alone.

2 Try to Avoid Falls

Falls can be a major problem, so make sure the living space the person is moving around has no rugs on the floor to trip them up and try to de-clutter. Eyesight problems such as cataracts can compromise their independence; so whilst they are still mobile and able to go for treatment it is worth getting eyes tested and glasses prescriptions updated. Comfortable foot ware is also important to stability. There are specialist shops that offer suitable foot ware.

3 Do Not Take Difficult Behaviour Personally

What they say to you or about you might be painful and difficult to hear at times. Just remember that it is the illness and they are not being deliberately uncooperative or hurtful. Just try not to take it to heart or feel rejected.

4 Try to Avoid Dehydration

Constipation can result from not drinking enough during the day.

Dehydration = constipation = increase in confused behaviour

Talk to your GP about this common problem as there are liquid preparations on prescription that can help. Urinary tract infections are also a problem for some; so always make sure they are encouraged to drink plenty of liquid. Using brightly coloured cups or drinking straws can help. If urinary tract infections become a problem you could consider sneaking cranberry extract into their diet in the form of fruit juice or dried pills.

5 Difficulties Swallowing

Difficulties swallowing food and liquid often develops with age and can be a particular problem in someone with dementia. It is an automatic reaction to stretch the neck forward and upwards if this happens. However if they drop their chin to their chest it actually opens up the throat and makes it easier to swallow. It is counter-intuitive; but worth a try to see if it helps.

6 Communication is Important

Make good use of a thick black felt pen and white card to make simple instructive labels you can put in prominent places around their living area. Also put a note pad with a pen tied to it in a prominent place so that messages can be left for district nurses and carers coming in. This gives them an easy way of writing down anything they need to tell you without having to search for pen and paper as they are often in such a hurry.

7 Identity Information

Make sure there is your name, telephone number, carers contact details and other important information on a card inside their handbag or wallet just in case they wander off at any time.

8 Baby wipes

Get a few packs and dot them around in strategic places as they are a godsend when cleaning up.

9 "Time Out" for You

Make sure you have definite plans for using any free time you get. Outings, and events run by local caring organisations are good for releasing some of your feelings with other people who understand your predicament. Also build in time for hobbies, interests and seeing friends as caring is a lonely isolating business.

10 Try Not to Feel Guilty

It isn't your fault they have become ill. Dark thought s are natural in your situation...so don't feel guilty about them!

Bibliography

Buddhism

"How to Become a Buddha in 5 Weeks – the simple way to self-realisation"
by Giulio Cesare Giacobbe

This is a fantastic little book crammed full of wisdom and an easy read compared to other books on Buddhism that I have found too complex to understand … my new bible of how to live a good life.

General interest to all carers

"The Selfish Pig's Guide to Caring"
by Hugh Marriott illustrated by David Lock

This book was lent to me by one of the people at my reading group … and I don't want to give it back! I had just let the cat out of the bag to the group regarding this book I'd written about caring for mum … she thought I need to see what I was up against in terms of competition!

Actually it is brilliantly written and illustrated and worth a read for anyone who is a carer as it tackles just about every subject with a wealth of information … and more importantly it is humorous and very honest on a personal level. It isn't about dementia as such; but most of the information is very relevant whatever the condition is of the person being cared for.

Dementia

"Dementia-The One-Stop Guide" Practical advice for families, professionals and people living with dementia and Alzheimer's disease"
by Professor June Andrews

This book is a good source of help to carers as it gives up to date research findings and advice regarding caring for someone with these diseases. It gives a more scientific and detached view of the subject. Well worth a read.